WORDS TO KNOW
KINDERGARTEN SIGHT WORDS

dog

Brighter Child®
Carson Dellosa Education
Greensboro, North Carolina

Brighter Child®
Carson Dellosa Education
PO Box 35665
Greensboro, NC 27425 USA

ISBN 978-1-4838-4932-4

Table of Contents

For Parents and Caregivers

This book will help your child learn to read and write 100 of the most commonly used words in the English language. Memorizing these words, or knowing them "by sight," will form a strong foundation for your child as he or she grows as a reader.

What Are Sight Words?

Sight words are words that children see often in books, on signs, at school, and everywhere! Sometimes called *high-frequency words*, *instant words*, or *core words*, these are the short words that make up much of what we read. It is estimated that the same 100 words or so make up more than half of all the words that students are expected to read. If that seems hard to believe, look at a page from any book. How many of the words on that page are common words like *the*, *was*, and *that*?

Some sight words cannot be sounded out using phonics rules. Or, they rely on rules that your child will learn later in school. Imagine trying to sound out each letter in words like *the*, *are*, and *said*. It doesn't work very well! Memorizing these words frees your child to concentrate on sounding out words that follow more predictable patterns.

Some sight words can be sounded out, but they are so common that it is an advantage to memorize them. Words like *did*, *mom*, and *look* appear frequently in children's books. With a little practice, your child will learn to read them at a glance.

Why Is It Important to Learn Sight Words?

Learning to read the words in this book "by sight" will greatly benefit your child as a new reader. First, learning sight words develops **confidence**. When your child looks at a book and already recognizes many words, he or she is more likely to keep reading. Second, knowing sight words promotes **reading comprehension**. Since your child will already know many words, he or she can focus on new words that are important to the meaning of a text. Finally, learning sight words will help your child develop **speed and fluency**. With so many words already memorized, reading is full speed ahead!

How Will This Book Help My Child Learn Sight Words?

This book features 100 sight words for kindergartners arranged in 10 sections according to their level of difficulty and some shared spelling and meaning patterns. Dip into the activities at any point—it is not necessary to go from front to back. The **tracing**, **writing**, **word recognition**, and **spelling activities** are short, predictable, and easy to do, providing the repeated practice that will help your child remember each word. A **review** at the end of each section includes sentences and stories. A complete set of **flash cards** is provided for hands-on practice.

How Can I Help My Child Learn Sight Words?

The activities in this book are a great starting point for helping your child learn sight words. Try these ideas for even more practice.

☐ Cut out the flash cards at the back of this book. See page 281 for creative suggestions for using the cards.

☐ Look for sight words on signs, menus, junk mail, and everywhere!

☐ Focus on one sight word. How many times can your child find it as you read a picture book together? Praise your child for reading the word!

☐ Use magnetic letters to spell sight words on the fridge or on a cookie sheet.

☐ Play hangman to reveal a sight word. Or, play tic-tac-toe, writing sight words in place of *X* and *O*.

☐ Write a sight word on a strip of construction paper. Staple it in a loop around your child's wrist. How many times during the day can your child spy the word?

☐ Use letter stamps, play dough, scented markers, sidewalk chalk, or other fun supplies to write sight words.

☐ Rainbow-write! Write a sight word at a large size. Have your child use crayons to trace it in every color of the rainbow.

☐ Choose several sight words. Use them to write a sentence or a story together. Try trading short notes, texts, or e-mails that use sight words.

☐ Write sight words with your finger in a cookie tray filled with salt or dry rice.

☐ Print out a story. Provide two or three highlighters of different colors, assigning a sight word to each color. Ask your child to highlight sight words in the story using the colors.

☐ Write sight words on masking tape pieces stuck to the floor around the room. Call out a sight word. Can your child run to the word and stand on it?

My List of 100 Words

Make a check mark beside each word you know how to read. If you need help, find the word's pages and practice again.

- [ ] **all** (pages 44–45)
- [ ] **am** (pages 36–37)
- [ ] **apple** (pages 182–183)
- [ ] **are** (pages 74–75)
- [ ] **at** (pages 16–17)
- [ ] **ate** (pages 168–169)
- [ ] **away** (pages 250–251)
- [ ] **ball** (pages 46–47)
- [ ] **be** (pages 18–19)
- [ ] **big** (pages 70–71)
- [ ] **black** (pages 178–179)
- [ ] **blue** (pages 104–105)
- [ ] **boat** (pages 102–103)
- [ ] **boy** (pages 72–73)
- [ ] **brown** (pages 180–181)
- [ ] **but** (pages 112–113)
- [ ] **came** (pages 192–193)
- [ ] **cat** (pages 22–23)
- [ ] **cow** (pages 166–167)
- [ ] **dad** (pages 66–67)
- [ ] **day** (pages 92–93)
- [ ] **did** (pages 38–39)
- [ ] **do** (pages 8–9)
- [ ] **dog** (pages 24–25)
- [ ] **doll** (pages 48–49)
- [ ] **down** (pages 224–225)
- [ ] **eat** (pages 120–121)
- [ ] **farm** (pages 172–173)
- [ ] **first** (pages 242–243)
- [ ] **four** (pages 142–143)
- [ ] **get** (pages 62–63)
- [ ] **girl** (pages 130–131)
- [ ] **go** (pages 12–13)
- [ ] **good** (pages 226–227)
- [ ] **green** (pages 148–149)
- [ ] **have** (pages 176–177)
- [ ] **he** (pages 60–61)
- [ ] **help** (pages 128–129)
- [ ] **here** (pages 200–201)
- [ ] **into** (pages 222–223)
- [ ] **jump** (pages 228–229)
- [ ] **like** (pages 156–157)
- [ ] **little** (pages 254–255)
- [ ] **look** (pages 124–125)
- [ ] **may** (pages 88–89)
- [ ] **mom** (pages 114–115)
- [ ] **must** (pages 52–53)
- [ ] **new** (pages 42–43)

☐ **no** (pages 10–11)
☐ **not** (pages 64–65)
☐ **now** (pages 86–87)
☐ **on** (pages 34–35)
☐ **orange** (pages 258–259)
☐ **our** (pages 98–99)
☐ **out** (pages 76–77)
☐ **over** (pages 216–217)
☐ **pig** (pages 164–165)
☐ **play** (pages 154–155)
☐ **please** (pages 260–261)
☐ **pretty** (pages 234–235)
☐ **purple** (pages 256–257)
☐ **ran** (pages 68–69)
☐ **red** (pages 40–41)
☐ **ride** (pages 100–101)
☐ **run** (pages 20–21)
☐ **said** (pages 246–247)
☐ **saw** (pages 26–27)
☐ **say** (pages 118–119)
☐ **school** (pages 208–209)
☐ **see** (pages 94–95)
☐ **she** (pages 122–123)
☐ **sheep** (pages 230–231)
☐ **so** (pages 14–15)
☐ **soon** (pages 198–199)

☐ **stop** (pages 194–195)
☐ **that** (pages 150–151)
☐ **the** (pages 96–97)
☐ **then** (pages 196–197)
☐ **there** (pages 202–203)
☐ **they** (pages 244–245)
☐ **this** (pages 126–127)
☐ **too** (pages 170–171)
☐ **toy** (pages 50–51)
☐ **tree** (pages 146–147)
☐ **under** (pages 152–153)
☐ **walk** (pages 252–253)
☐ **want** (pages 174–175)
☐ **was** (pages 116–117)
☐ **well** (pages 140–141)
☐ **went** (pages 218–219)
☐ **what** (pages 248–249)
☐ **when** (pages 144–145)
☐ **where** (pages 204–205)
☐ **white** (pages 232–233)
☐ **who** (pages 78–79)
☐ **will** (pages 138–139)
☐ **with** (pages 220–221)
☐ **yellow** (pages 206–207)
☐ **yes** (pages 190–191)
☐ **you** (pages 90–91)

do

READ the word. **SAY** it out loud.

What kind **do** you want?

TRACE and **WRITE** the word.

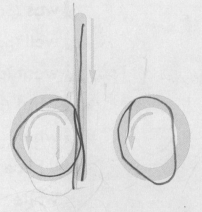

FIND the word. Color the cherries with **do**.

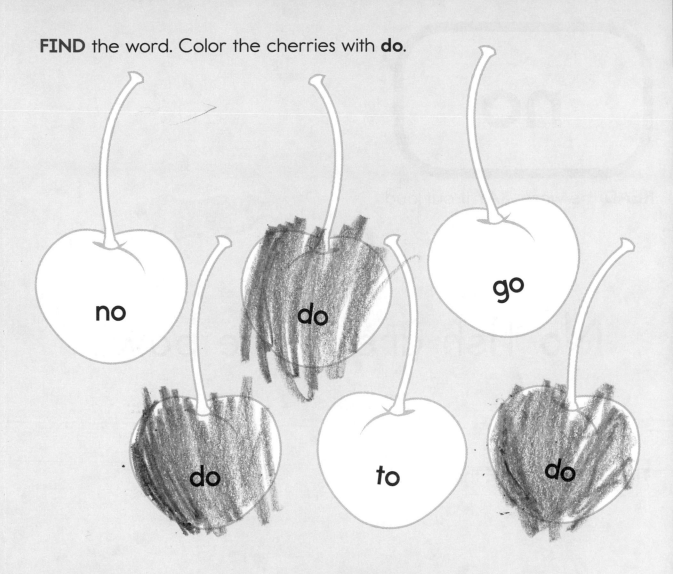

SPELL the word. Write the missing letters.

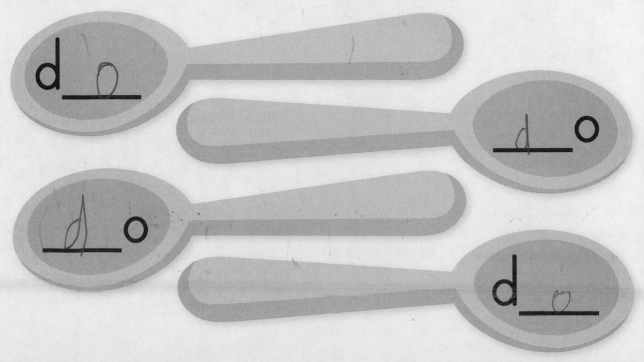

no

READ the word. **SAY** it out loud.

No fish are in the bowl.

TRACE and **WRITE** the word.

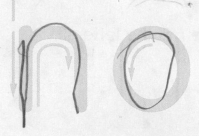

FIND the word. Color the spaces with **no**.

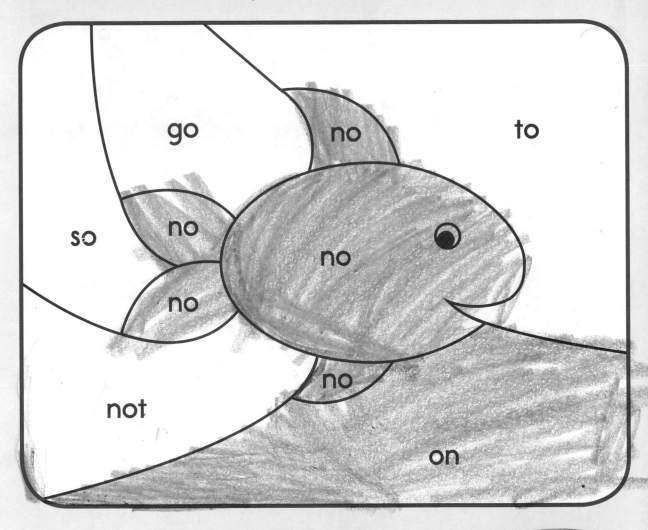

SPELL the word. Circle the letters in **no**.

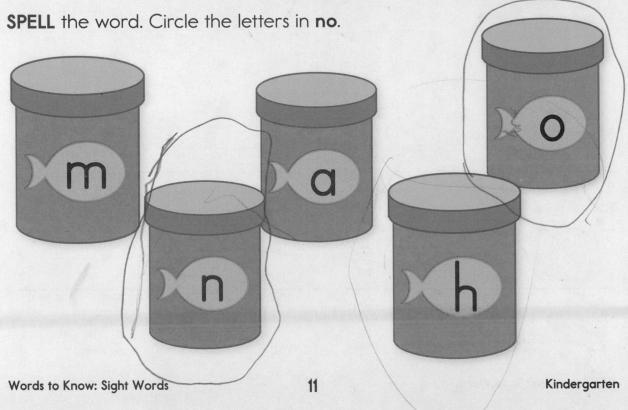

READ the word. **SAY** it out loud.

Trains go over the tracks.

TRACE and **WRITE** the word.

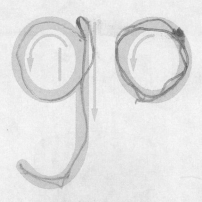

---

go go go

FIND the word. Circle each train car with the letters in **go**.

FIND the word. Color **go** on each sign.

SO

READ the word. **SAY** it out loud.

I am **so** sleepy.

TRACE and **WRITE** the word.

so

- -

so

FIND the word. Circle **so**.

FIND the word. Color the spaces with **so** yellow. Color the other spaces black.

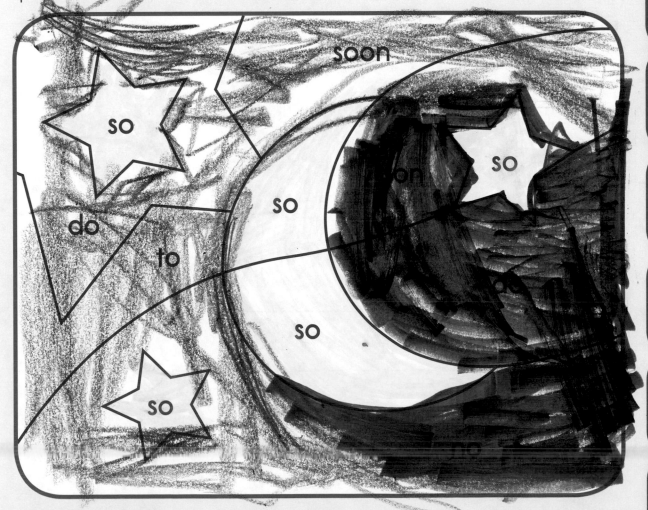

Words to Know: Sight Words

Kindergarten

at

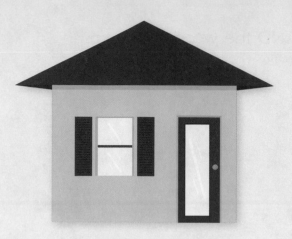

READ the word. **SAY** it out loud.

We stayed **at** home.

TRACE and **WRITE** the word.

at

FIND the word. Color the cars with **at**.

FIND the word. Draw a line through the path with **at**.

be

READ the word. **SAY** it out loud.

Will it **be** a rainy day?

TRACE and **WRITE** the word.

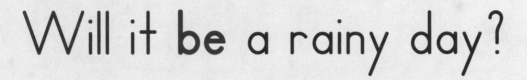

be

FIND the word. Color the spaces with **be**.

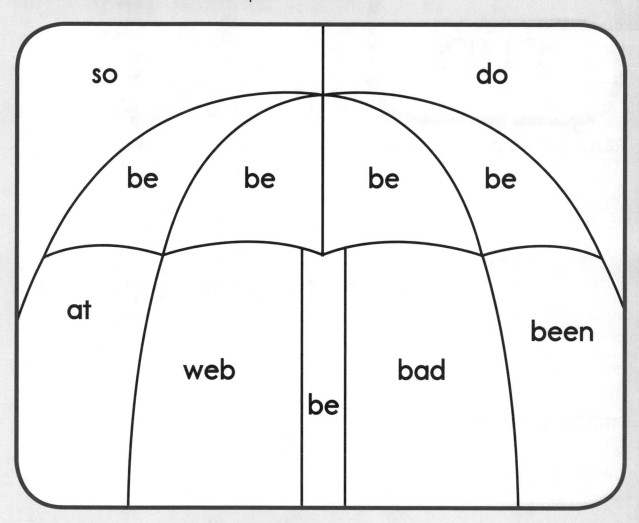

SPELL the word. Write the missing letters.

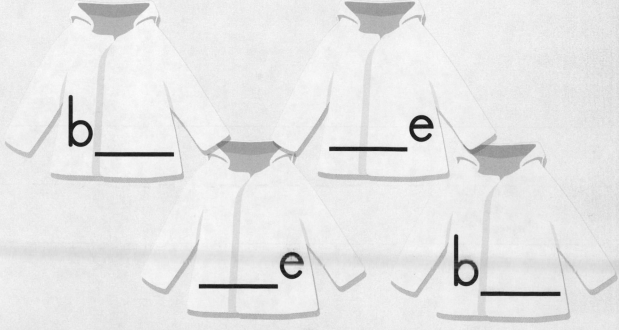

run

READ the word. **SAY** it out loud.

They **run** every day.

TRACE and **WRITE** the word.

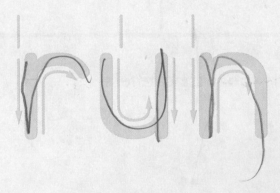

FIND the word. Color the shoes with **run**.

run

bun

sun

run

run

fun

FIND the word. See who wins the race. Circle **run**.

run   rug   run   fun   bun   FINISH

run   fun   ran   run   run   FINISH

up
no
go
so
at
be
run
cat
dog
saw

cat

READ the word. **SAY** it out loud.

I love my **cat**.

TRACE and **WRITE** the word.

cat

cat

FIND the word. Color the paw prints with **cat**.

cat

cat

cap

cat

can

bat

FIND the word. Circle **cat** in each row.

c a t h e

g c a t y

p c a t k

u l c a t

dog

READ the word. **SAY** it out loud.

My **dog** has spots.

TRACE and **WRITE** the word.

dog dogdg

FIND the word. Color the spaces with **dog**.

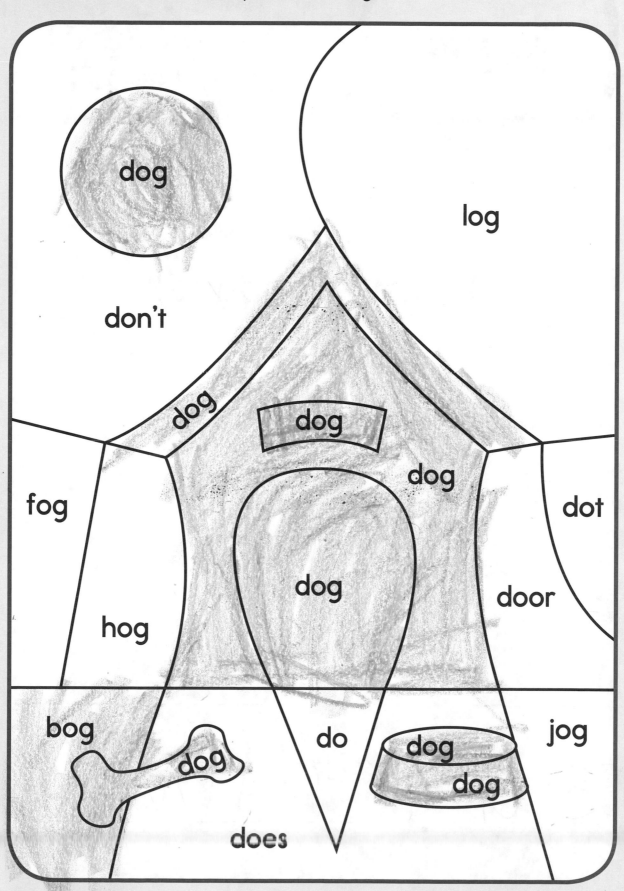

dog

log

don't

dog

dog

dog

fog

dog

dot

door

hog

dog

bog

dog

do

dog

dog

jog

does

do no go so at be run cat dog saw

saw

READ the word. **SAY** it out loud.

I **saw** a mouse!

TRACE and **WRITE** the word.

saw

saw saw

do
no
go
so
at
be
run
cat
dog
saw

FIND the word. Circle **saw**.

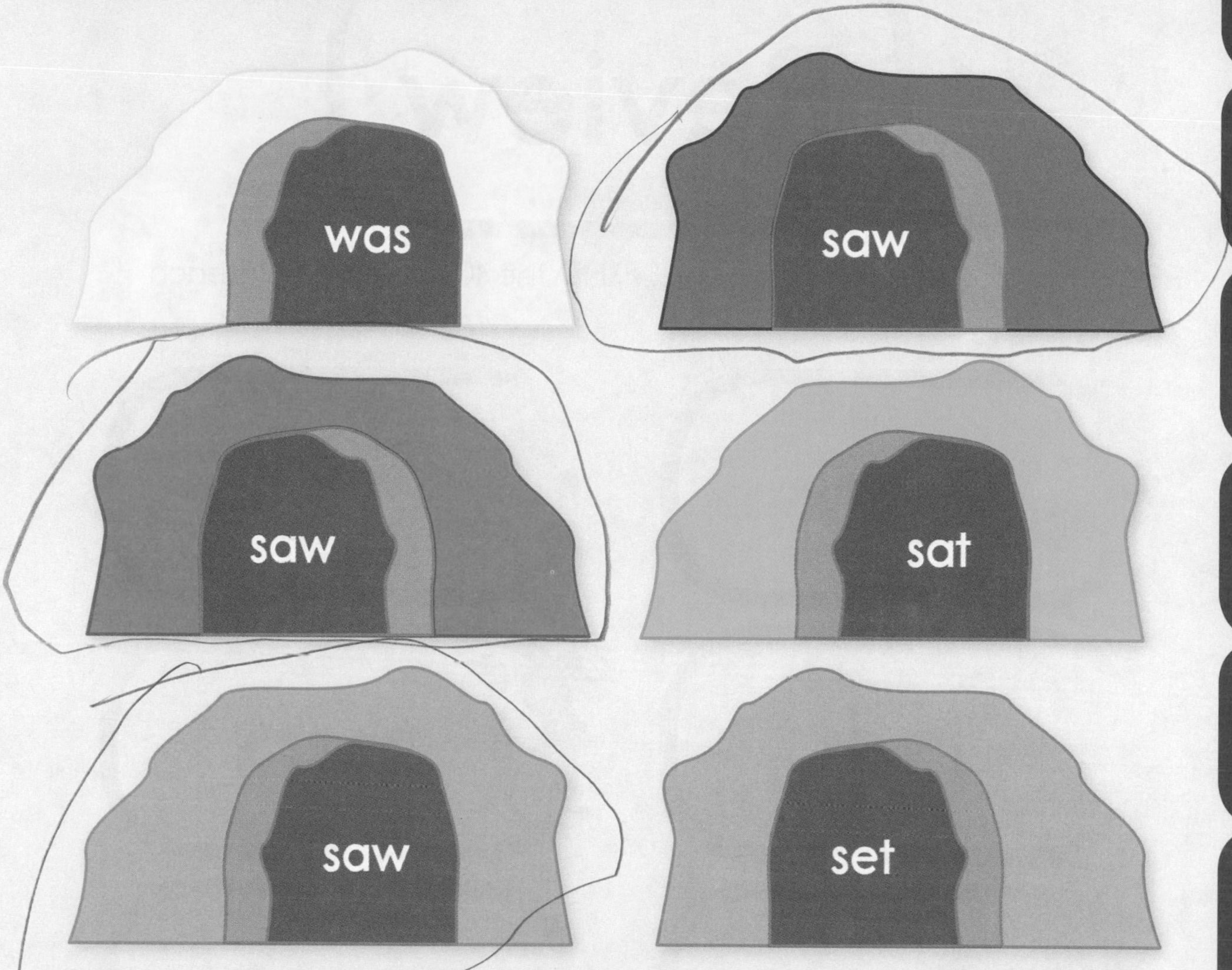

was

saw

saw

sat

saw

set

SPELL the word. Write the missing letters.

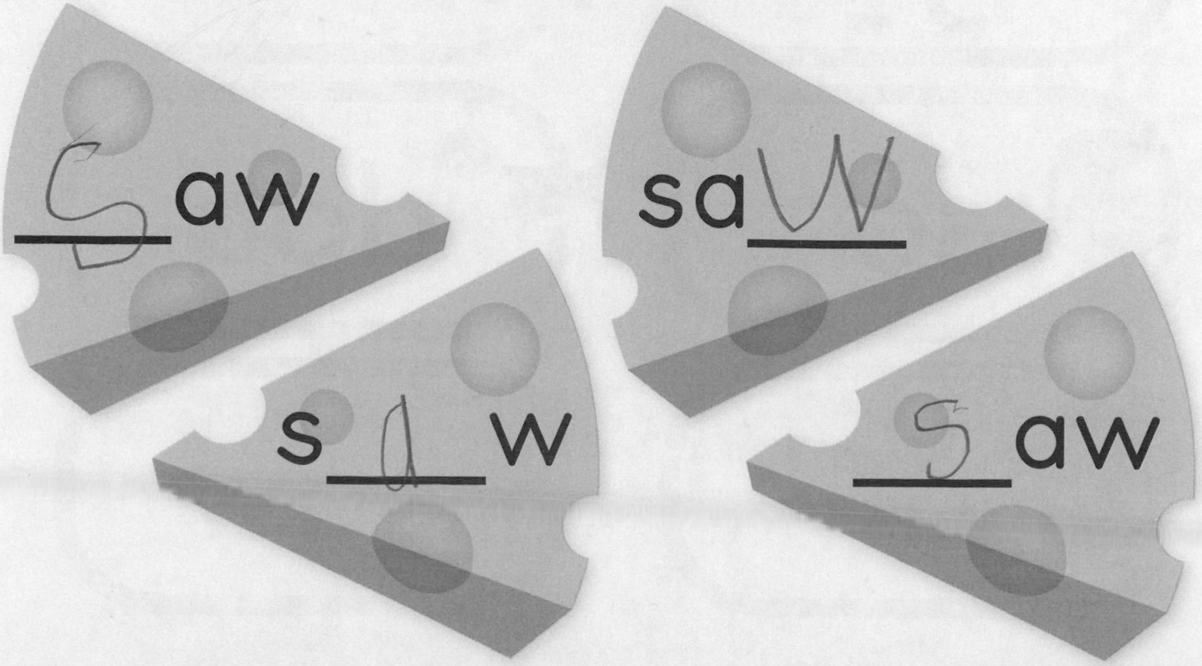

_S_aw

sa_w_

s_a_w

_S_aw

Review

READ the story on the next page. FIND the 10 words. Circle each word you find.

do

be

no

run

go

cat

so

dog

at

saw

Review

My Funny Pets

My pets are so funny. They do love to play. My cat will be hiding. She waits for my dog to go by. When my dog is at the spot, my cat jumps out! Then, my dog will run!

My cat has no idea what is coming. While she sleeps, my dog drops a toy on her paw. She wakes up and they both run! It is the funniest thing you ever saw.

do
no
go
so
at
be
run
cat
dog
saw

Review

WRITE words to finish the sentences.

at	so	run	dog	go

This apple is _____ good!

The bus is _____ the corner.

Mom will _____ in a race.

Can we _____ to Grandma's?

Why did the _____ bark?

do

no

go

so

at

be

run

cat

dog

saw

Review

WRITE words to finish the sentences.

be	do	cat	no	saw

_____

I _____ a full moon.

_____

I can _____ a cartwheel.

_____

This movie can _____ scary.

_____

Does your _____ have stripes?

_____

There is _____ salad left.

Review

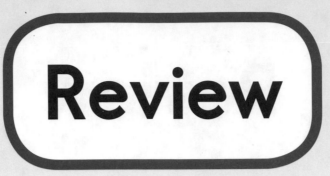

COLOR the words. Use the code.

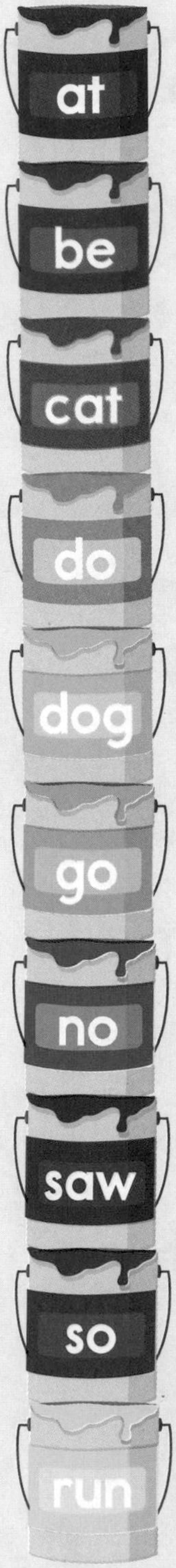
at
be
cat
do
dog
go
no
saw
so
run

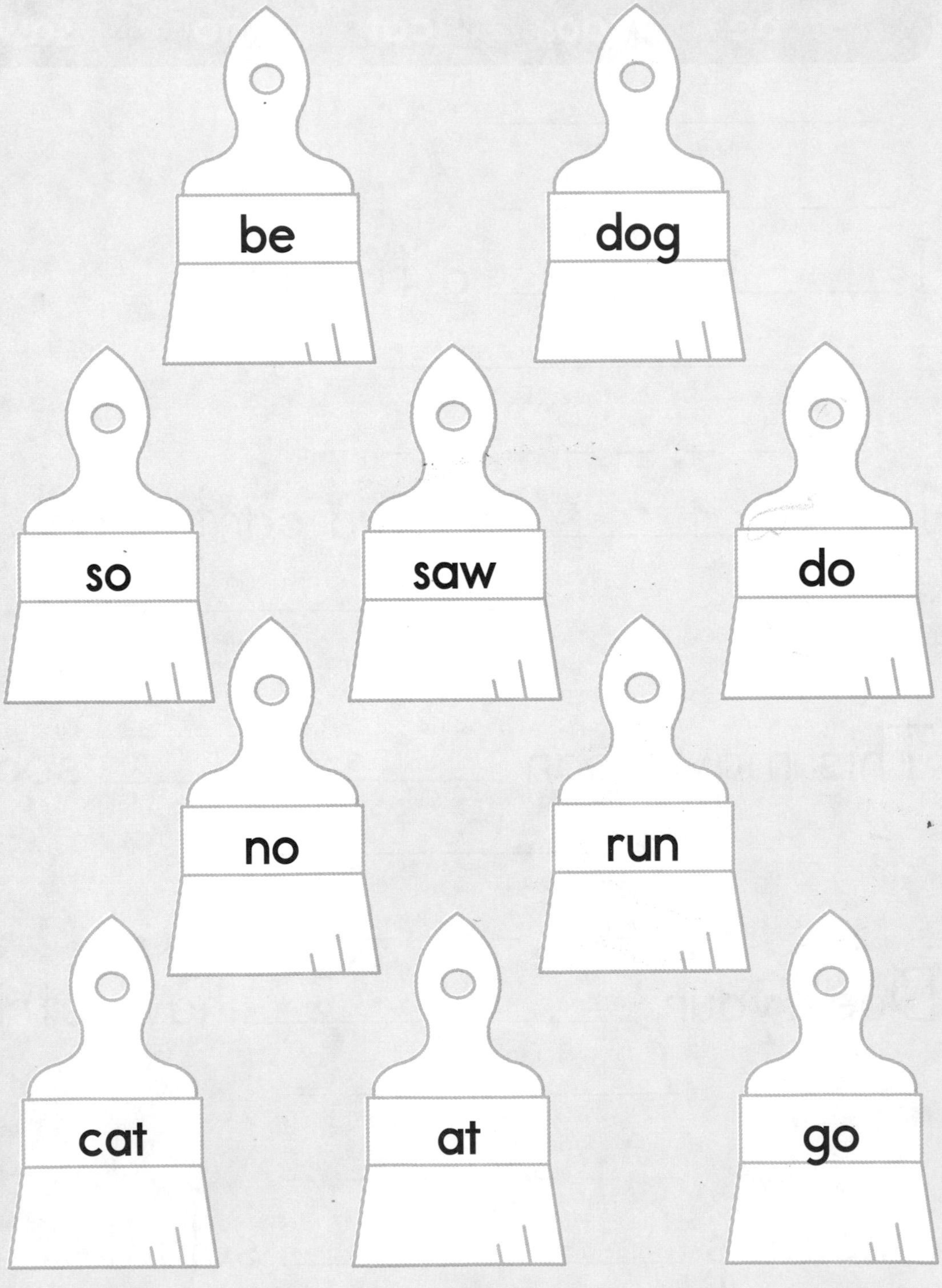
be
dog
so
saw
do
no
run
cat
at
go

Review

FIND the words in the puzzle. Look → and ↓.

cat dog run saw at be do go no so

s	s	l	u	e	u	z	r	b	o
m	o	n	j	w	x	w	b	g	q
o	s	c	d	b	p	t	e	o	e
y	f	s	a	w	x	e	r	x	q
v	f	b	a	e	n	x	y	t	a
d	o	f	t	i	o	m	r	t	w
d	o	g	f	h	b	m	z	r	a
q	v	x	g	c	r	r	r	b	z
h	x	u	c	a	e	u	f	v	z
a	v	a	n	t	n	n	i	p	

on

am

did

red

new

all

ball

doll

toy

must

on

READ the word. **SAY** it out loud.

Candles are on the cake.

TRACE and **WRITE** the word.

on

FIND the word. Circle **on**.

FIND the word. Draw a line through **on** to see if you won!

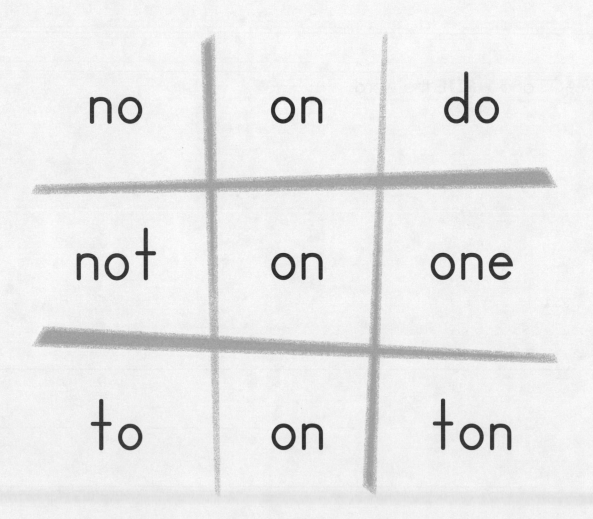

on

am

did

red

new

all

ball

doll

toy

must

on
am
did
red
new
all
ball
doll
toy
must

READ the word. **SAY** it out loud.

I am happy.

TRACE and **WRITE** the word.

am

FIND the word. Color the spaces with **am**.

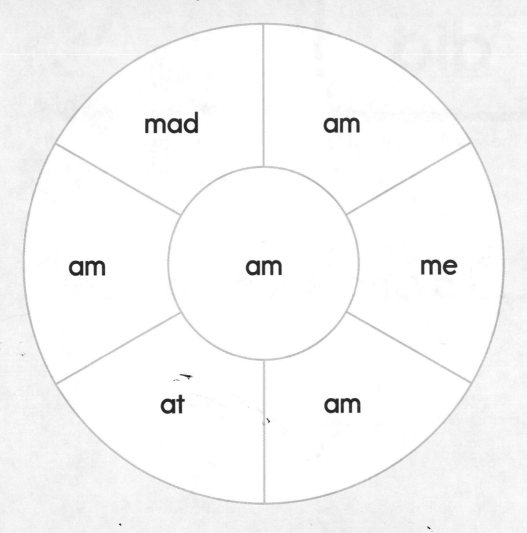

SPELL the word. Write the missing letters.

on
am
did
red
new
all
ball
doll
toy
must

on
am
did
red
new
all
ball
doll
toy
must

did

READ the word. **SAY** it out loud.

Did she score a goal?

TRACE and **WRITE** the word.

did

FIND the word. Draw a line through the path with **did**.

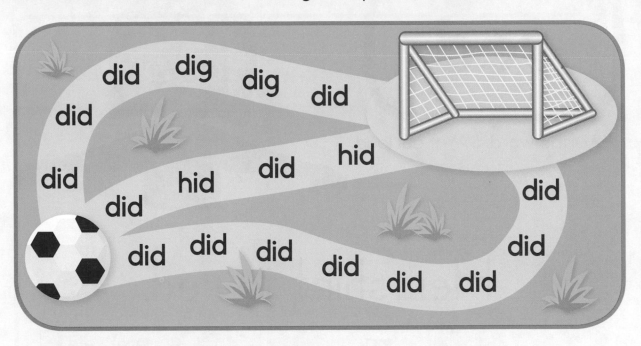

SPELL the word. Unscramble the letters to write **did**.

idd

ddi

ddi

idd

on
am
did
red
new
all
ball
doll
toy
must

on
am
did
red
new
all
ball
doll
toy
must

red

READ the word. **SAY** it out loud.

Her shirt is red.

TRACE and **WRITE** the word.

red

FIND the word. Use a red crayon to color the spaces with **red**.

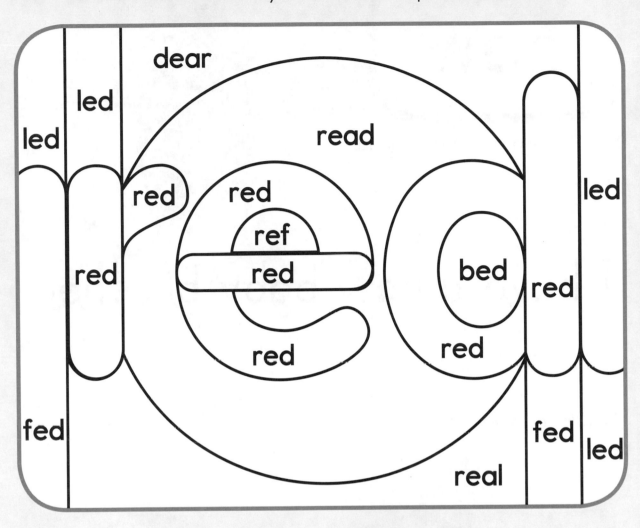

SPELL the word. Unscramble the letters to write **red**.

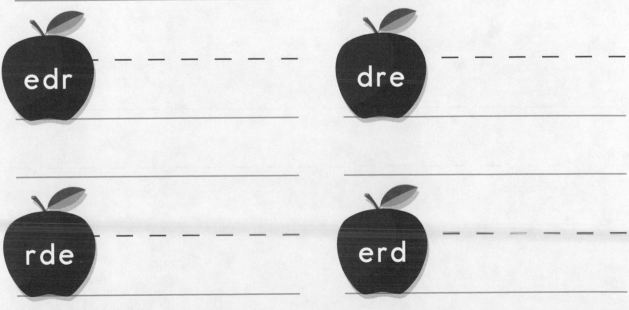

on
am
did
red
doll
new
all
ball
doll
toy
must

new

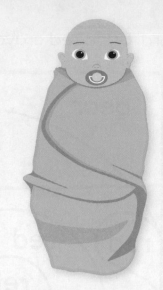

READ the word. **SAY** it out loud.

I have a **new** baby brother.

TRACE and **WRITE** the word.

new

_____

new _ _ _ _ _ _ _ _ _ _ _ _ _ _ _ _

FIND the word in the puzzle. Look ➜ and ↓.

n	e	w	m	y
r	p	n	e	w
n	n	e	n	a
y	e	w	s	z
j	w	e	n	g

FIND the word. Circle **new**.

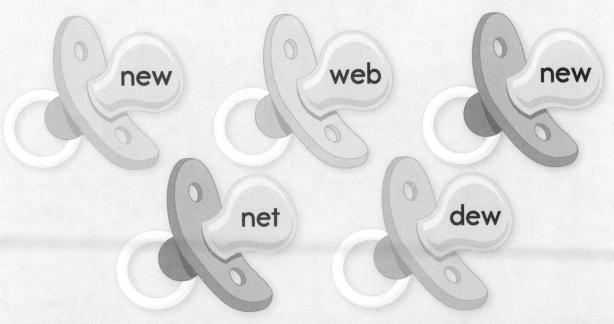

new   web   new

net   dew

on
am
did
red
new
all
ball
doll
toy
must

on
am
did
red
new
all
ball
doll
toy
must

all

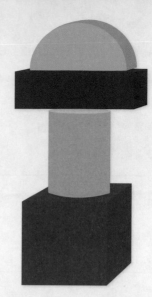

READ the word. **SAY** it out loud.

I used all the blocks.

TRACE and **WRITE** the word.

all

FIND the word. Draw a line through **all** to see if you won!

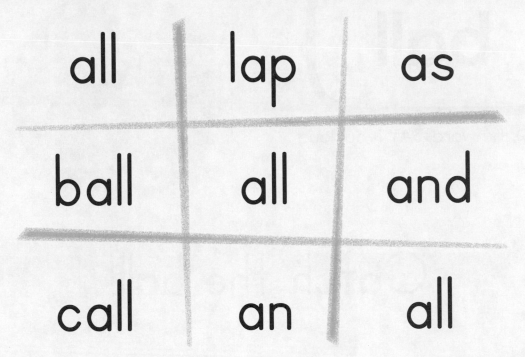

all	lap	as
ball	all	and
call	an	all

SPELL the word. Complete the word pyramids.

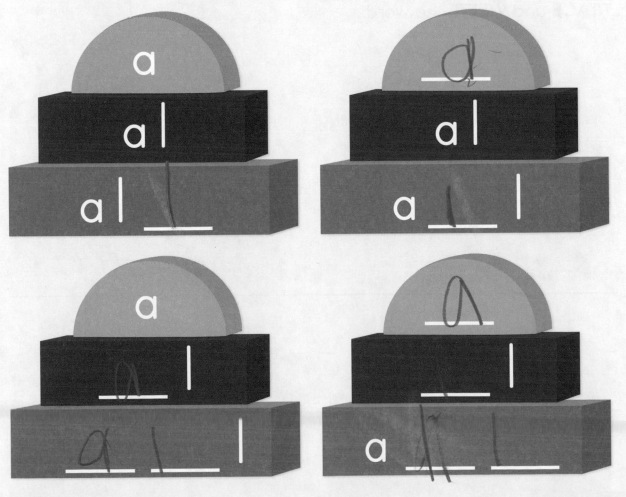

on
am
did
red
new
all
ball
doll
toy
must

on
am
did
red
new
all
ball
doll
toy
must

ball

READ the word. **SAY** it out loud.

Catch the ball!

TRACE and **WRITE** the word.

FIND the word. Color the spaces with **ball**.

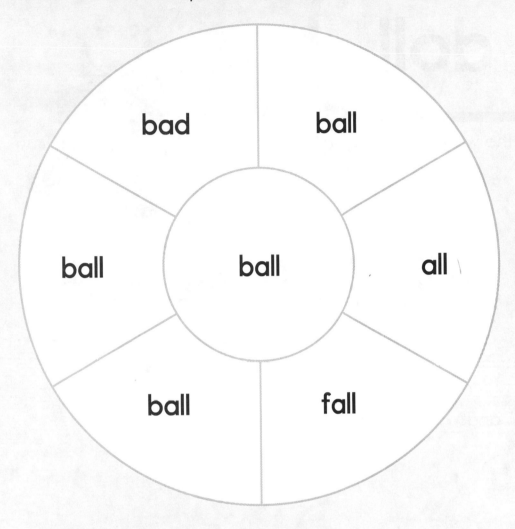

SPELL the word. Connect the letters in **ball**.

a•   •|

b•————————|

Words to Know: Sight Words

47

Kindergarten

on
am
did
red
new
all
ball
doll
toy
must

doll

READ the word. **SAY** it out loud.

My doll is dressed.

TRACE and **WRITE** the word.

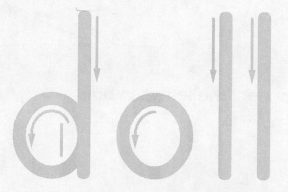

FIND the word in the puzzle. Look ➡ and ⬇.

y	r	m	d	d
e	h	b	o	o
k	d	o	l	l
d	o	l	l	l
q	c	b	d	j

SPELL the word. On each brush, circle the letters in **doll**.

b d e o l l

d a o l l

d o h l t l

p d o l l t

on
am
did
red
new
all
ball
doll
toy
must

toy

READ the word. **SAY** it out loud.

Which toy do you like best?

TRACE and **WRITE** the word.

FIND the word. Circle **toy**.

SPELL the word. Write the missing letters.

on
am
did
red
new
all
ball
doll
toy
must

on

am

did

red

new

all

ball

doll

toy

must

must

READ the word. **SAY** it out loud.

The pie must cool down.

TRACE and **WRITE** the word.

pie

FIND the word. Draw a line through the path with **must**.

must	must	must
must	must	must
most	must	must
must	must	must
most	must	must
must	must	must
most	mush	must
must	mush	must
must		must

on
am
did
red
new
all
ball
doll
toy
must

Review

READ the story on the next page. FIND the 10 words. Circle each word you find.

 **on**

 **all**

 **am**

 **ball**

 **did**

 **doll**

 **red**

 **toy**

 **new**

 **must**

Review

All My Work

I did jobs at home. I took out all the trash. I set plates on the table. Our dog must be fed each day. I am the one who feeds him. I got paid for all my work.

Now, I can buy a new toy. I can get a doll or a red ball. What do I want most? I cannot decide!

on
am
did
red
new
all
ball
doll
toy
must

Review

WRITE words to finish the sentences.

| am | did | ball | new | toy |

_____

The keys are the baby's _____.

Throw the _____ to me.

I got a _____ book to read.

_____ you eat lunch yet?

I _____ six years old.

Review

WRITE words to finish the sentences.

on	all	doll	must	red

b _ _ _ _ _ _

The fire truck is _____.

_ _ _ _ _ _ _ _

We ate _____ the popcorn.

_ _ _ _ _ _ _

Put your coat _____.

_ _ _ _ _ _ _ _

I _____ water the flowers.

_ _ _ _ _ _ _

The _____ has a pink dress.

on
am
did
red
new
all
ball
doll
toy
must

he

get

not

dad

ran

big

boy

are

out

who

he

READ the word. SAY it out loud.

He is our teacher.

TRACE and WRITE the word.

he

FIND the word. Color the spaces with **he**.

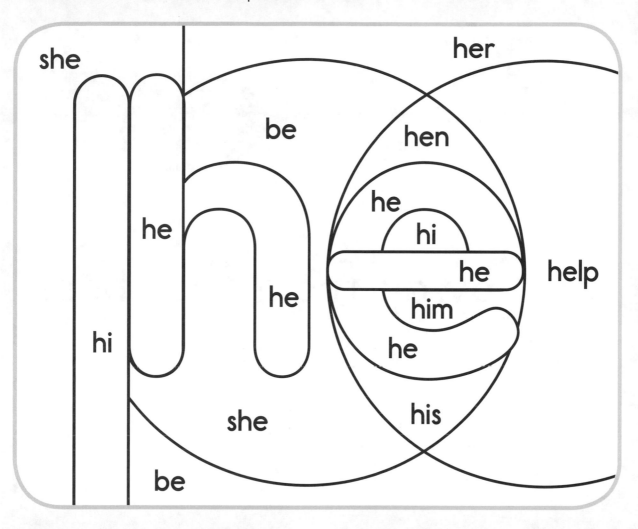

she
her
be
hen
he
he
hi
help
he
him
he
hi
she
his
be

FIND the word. Circle **he** in each row.

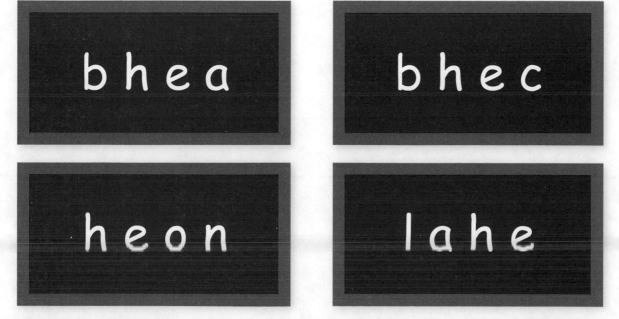

bhea

bhec

heon

lahe

he
get
not
dad
ran
big
boy
are
out
who

get

READ the word. SAY it out loud.

Get away from that bee!

TRACE and WRITE the word.

get

get

62

FIND the word. Circle **get**.

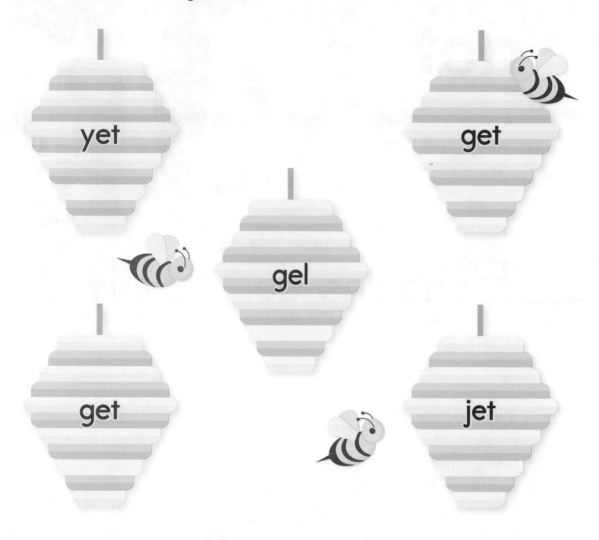

SPELL the word. Unscramble the letters to write **get**.

he
get
not
dad
ran
big
boy
are
out
who

he
get
not
dad
ran
big
boy
are
out
who

not

READ the word. SAY it out loud.

Penguins do not fly.

TRACE and WRITE the word.

not

FIND the word in the puzzle. Look → and ↓.

x	r	o	q	n
n	o	t	b	o
e	c	n	f	t
d	n	o	t	y
g	q	t	m	u

FIND the word. Cross out **not** to make each sentence true.

Penguins do not swim under water.

They do not have black and white feathers.

Penguins do not lay eggs.

dad

READ the word. **SAY** it out loud.

My dad holds my hand.

TRACE and **WRITE** the word.

dad

dad

he

get

not

dad

ran

big

boy

are

out

who

FIND the word. Draw a line through **dad** to see if you won!

add	did	bad
and	do	had
dad	dad	dad

FIND the word. Match the caps with **dad**.

he
get
not
dad
ran
big
boy
are
out
who

he
get
not
dad
ran
big
boy
are
out
who

ran

READ the word. SAY it out loud.

The rabbit ran in the yard.

TRACE and WRITE the word.

ran - - - - - - - - - - -

FIND the word. Circle **ran** on each tree.

run
ran
red

fan
man
ran

ran
sand
an

ban
ran
are

SPELL the word. Write the missing letters.

___an

r___n

ra___

he
get
not
dad
ran
big
boy
are
out
who

he

get

not

dad

ran

big

boy

are

out

who

big

READ the word. **SAY** it out loud.

Elephants are big.

TRACE and **WRITE** the word.

big

big

FIND the word. Draw a line through the path with **big**.

big   big

big

big

big

big

big

big

pig

big

big

big

big

big

big

big

big

big

big

big

big

big

big

big

big

big

bib

big

pig

he
get
not
dad
ran
big
boy
are
out
who

he

get

not

dad

ran

big

boy

are

out

who

boy

READ the word. **SAY** it out loud.

The boy waved to me.

TRACE and **WRITE** the word.

FIND the word. Color the spaces with **boy**.

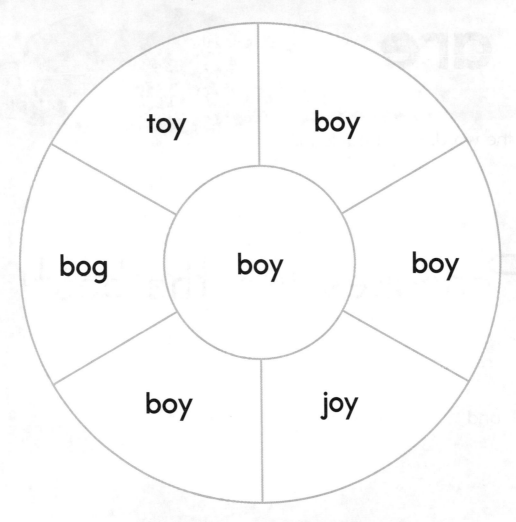

toy   boy

bog   boy   boy

boy   joy

SPELL the word. Complete the word pyramids.

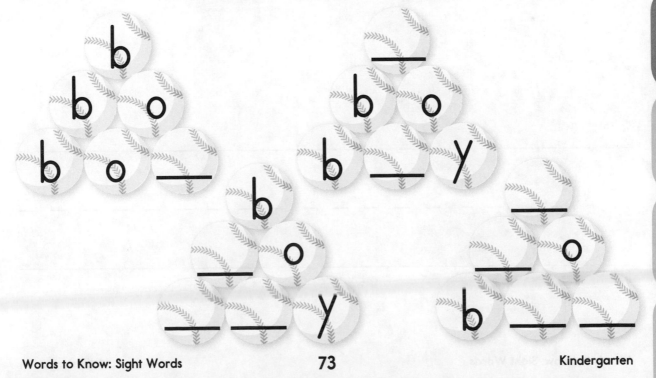

are

READ the word. SAY it out loud.

Pancakes are the best!

TRACE and WRITE the word.

_____

are -- -- -- -- -- -- -- --

FIND the word in the puzzle. Look → and ↓.

m	c	a	r	e
e	c	r	y	m
z	l	e	p	a
n	x	r	k	r
a	r	e	v	e

SPELL the word. Unscramble the letters to write **are**.

rea _____

ear _____

aer _____

rae _____

he
get
not
dad
ran
big
boy
are
out
who

he

get

not

dad

ran

big

boy

are

out

who

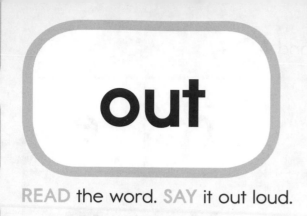

out

READ the word. SAY it out loud.

The fish is out of the water.

TRACE and WRITE the word.

out

FIND the word. Circle **out**.

SPELL the word. In each row, circle the letters in **out**.

he
get
not
dad
ran
big
boy
are
out
who

he
get
not
dad
ran
big
boy
are
out
who

who

READ the word. SAY it out loud.

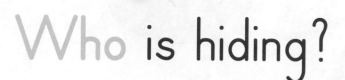

Who is hiding?

TRACE and WRITE the word.

who

FIND the word. Color the spaces with **who**.

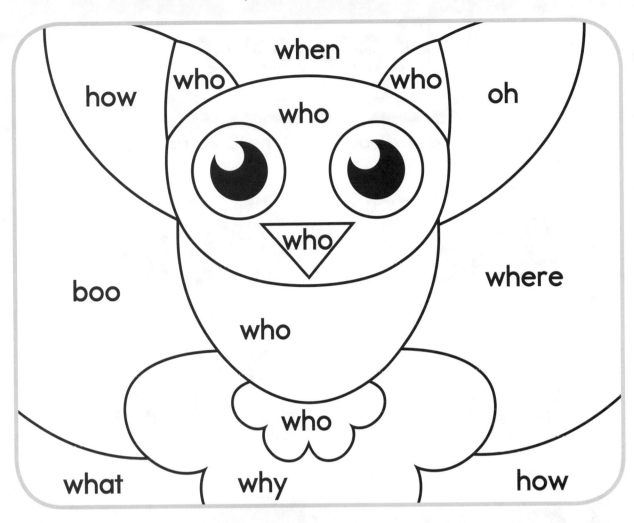

SPELL the word. Write the missing letters.

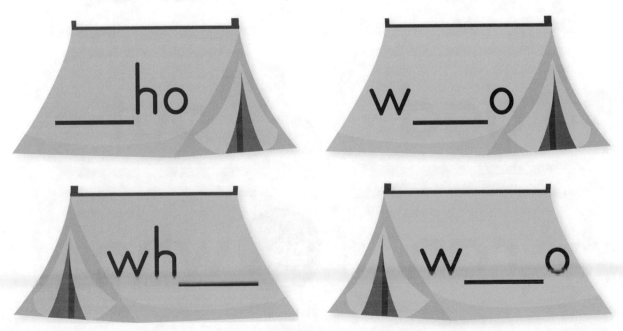

he

get

not

dad

ran

big

boy

are

out

who

he
get
not
dad
ran
big
boy
are
out
who

Review

READ the story on the next page. **FIND** the 10 words. Circle each word you find.

 he

 big

 get

 boy

 not

 are

 dad

 out

 ran

 who

Words to Know: Sight Words

Kindergarten

Review

Who Is Next?

Gabe ran behind the shed. The boy held something big and wobbly. His hand bumped the wall. "Who is there?" Gabe's dad called.

Gabe did not make another sound. He did not want his dad to find him.

Gabe's dad came closer. Then, Gabe jumped out and tossed the wobbly thing high. The water balloon burst. His dad got all wet, but he had a big smile.

"You are going to be the next one to get wet!" his dad laughed.

he
get
not
dad
ran
big
boy
are
out
who

he
get
not
dad
ran
big
boy
are
out
who

Review

WRITE words to finish the sentences.

get	boy	out	not	ran

_ _ _ _ _ _ _ _

Can we _____ pizza for dinner?

_ _ _ _ _ _ _ _

It is _____ time to go yet.

_ _ _ _ _ _ _ _

We _____ as fast as we could.

_ _ _ _ _ _ _ _

Oliver is a _____ in my class.

_ _ _ _ _ _ _ _

Fluffy got _____ of his cage.

Review

WRITE words to finish the sentences.

who	big	dad	he	are

_____

The red ball is _____.

_____

I have to ask my _____.

_____ wants to play?

_____ lost his coat.

_____

We _____ late for the show.

he get not dad ran big boy are out who

Review

SORT the words. Write each word on the balloon that shows its vowel letter. You will write two words on two different balloons.

he get not dad ran big boy are out who

Words with **a**
dad
ran
are

Words with **e**
he
get

Word with **i**
big

Words with **o**
boy
not
who

Word with **u**
out

Words to Know: Sight Words

84

Kindergarten

Review

GRAPH the words. Color one box for each word you count.

boy   who   are   big   are

get   out   he   dad   he

ran   not   get   who   are

out   boy   he   out

are   he   are   not   get

big					
not					
out					
who					
are					
get					
ran					
he					
dad					
boy					

now
may
you
day
see
the
our
ride
boat
blue

now

READ the word. SAY it out loud.

What time is it now?

TRACE and WRITE the word.

now

FIND the word. Color the spaces with **now**.

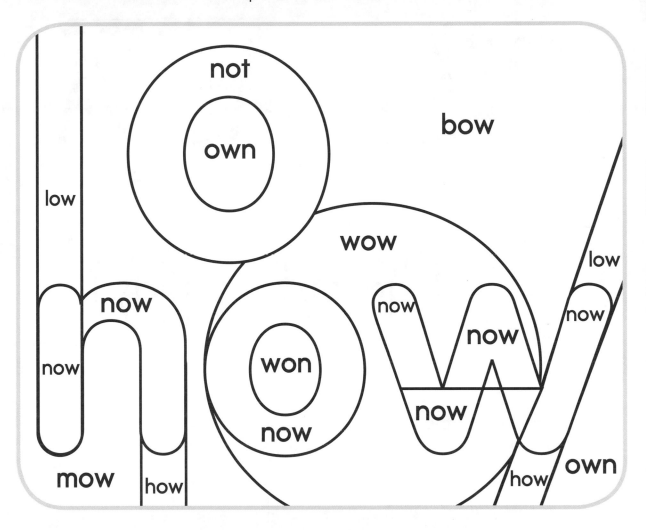

SPELL the word. Unscramble the letters to write **now**.

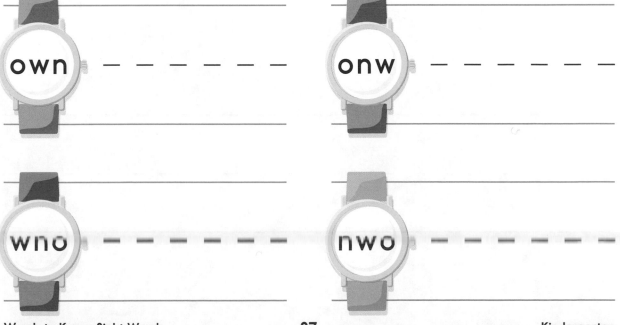

now   may   you   day   see   the   our   ride   boat   blue

now

may

you

day

see

the

our

ride

boat

blue

may

READ the word. SAY it out loud.

May I go out to play?

TRACE and WRITE the word.

may

FIND the word in the puzzle. Look → and ↓.

h	i	t	x	a
t	i	m	a	y
m	m	a	y	m
a	r	e	e	a
y	q	j	r	y

SPELL the word. On each slide, circle the letters in **may**.

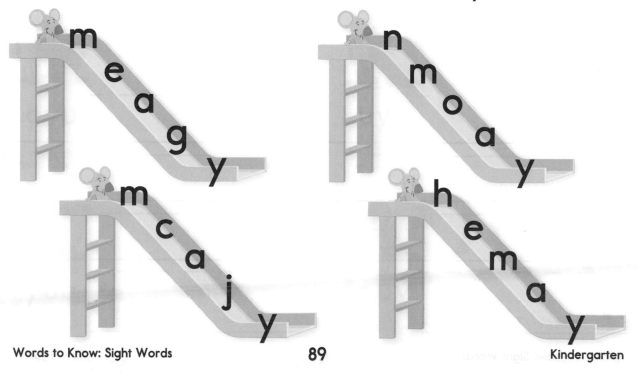

m e a g y

n n m o a y

m c a j y

h e m a y

now

may

you

day

see

the

our

ride

boat

blue

now

may

you

day

see

the

our

ride

boat

blue

day

READ the word. SAY it out loud.

I had a good day at school.

TRACE and WRITE the word.

day

FIND the word. Color the spaces with **day**.

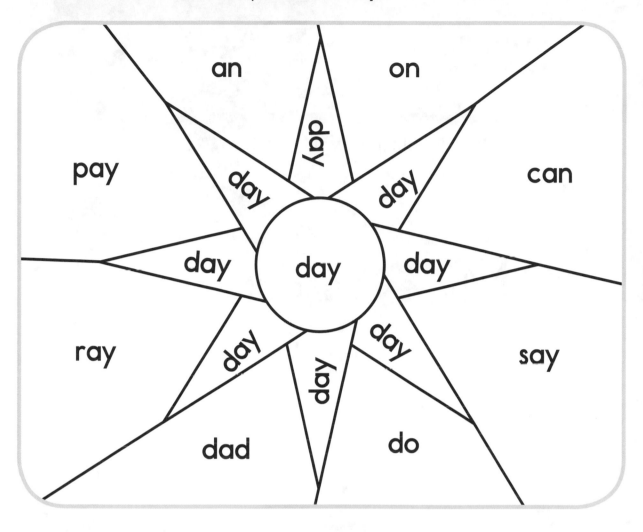

SPELL the word. Write the missing letters.

da____

d____y

____ay

da____

now
may
you
day
see
the
our
ride
boat
blue

now

may

you

day

see

the

our

ride

boat

blue

see

READ the word. SAY it out loud.

My eyes can see.

TRACE and WRITE the word.

see

FIND the word. Circle **see**.

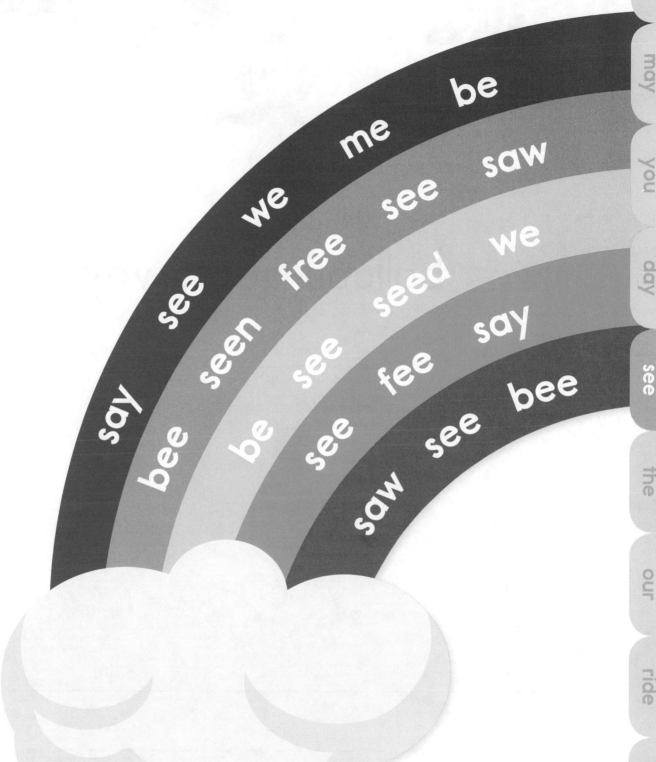

now
may
you
day
see
the
our
ride
boat
blue

now
may
you
day
see
the
our
ride
boat
blue

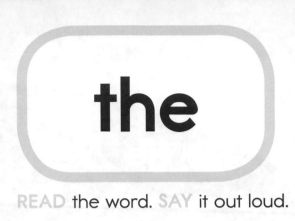

the

READ the word. SAY it out loud.

The balloon got away!

TRACE and WRITE the word.

the

FIND the word. Color the spaces with **the**.

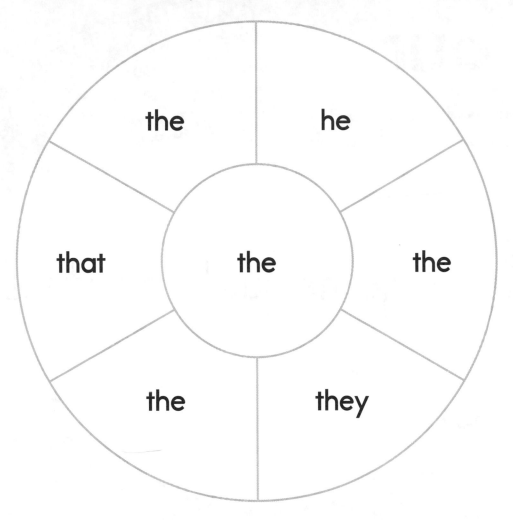

SPELL the word. Write the missing letters.

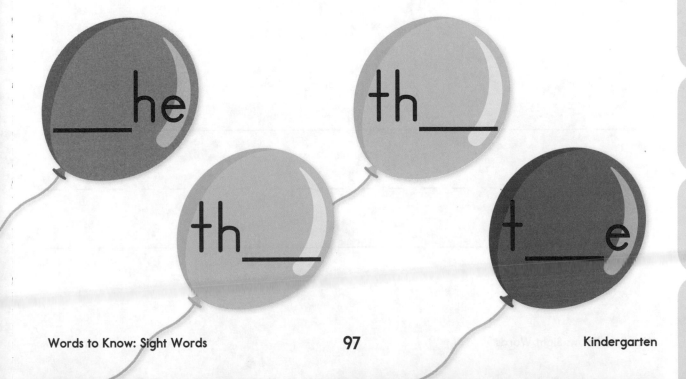

our

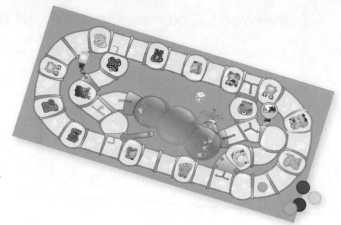

READ the word. SAY it out loud.

Our game just started.

TRACE and WRITE the word.

our

our

FIND the word. Circle **our** to see who wins the game.

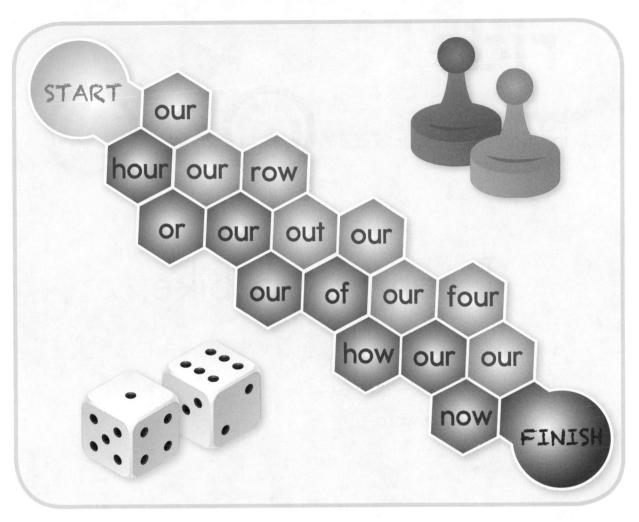

SPELL the word. Complete the word pyramids.

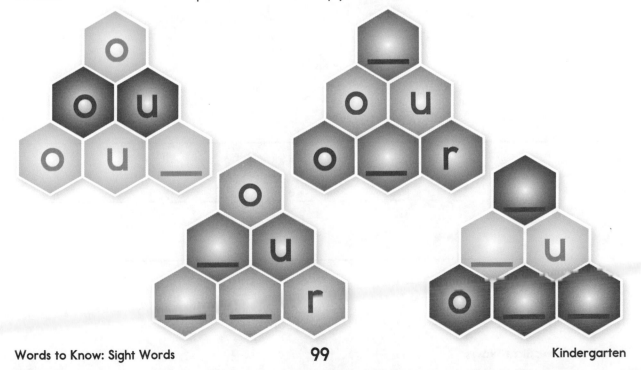

now
may
you
day
see
the
our
ride
boat
blue

now
may
you
day
see
the
our
ride
boat
blue

ride

READ the word. SAY it out loud.

I can ride a bike.

TRACE and WRITE the word.

ride

ride

COLOR each box with **ride**. Match each number to a letter to answer the riddle.

	e	r	i	t	d
5	rid	hide	wide	ripe	ride
4	ride	rise	deer	ear	tide
3	are	ride	ripe	red	rise
2	deer	tide	ride	rid	are
1	hide	ear	red	ride	wide

Why does a bike not stand up on its own?

Because it is too ___ ___ ___ ___ ___!
         1   2   3   4   5

now
may
you
day
see
the
our
ride
boat
blue

now

may

you

day

see

the

our

ride

boat

blue

boat

READ the word. SAY it out loud.

Dock the boat here.

TRACE and WRITE the word.

boat

FIND the word. Circle **boat**.

SPELL the word. Connect the letters in **boat**.

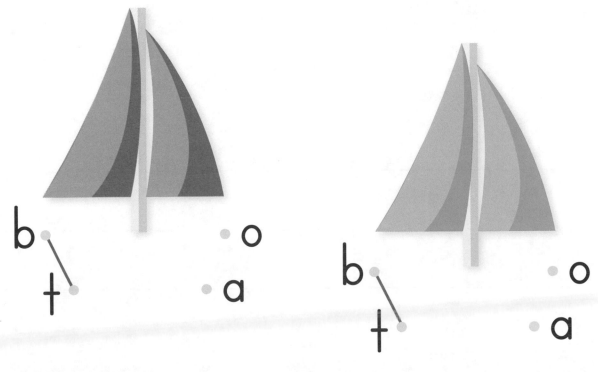

now

may

you

day

see

the

our

ride

boat

blue

now

may

you

day

see

the

our

ride

boat

blue

blue

READ the word. SAY it out loud.

The butterfly is blue.

TRACE and WRITE the word.

blue

blue

FIND the word. Use a blue crayon to color each bird in a nest with **blue**.

blue

blew

black

blue

SPELL the word. On each paint stroke, circle the letters in **blue**.

b h l u a e

b l n u e c

d b t l u e

p b l o u e

Review

READ the program on the next page. FIND the 10 words. Circle each word you find.

 now

 the

 may

 our

 you

 ride

 day

 boat

 see

 blue

Review

School Fun Day
Saturday, April 26

12:00: Sing-Along with "Row, Row, Row Your Boat"

1:00: Tours to See the Garden at Our School

2:00: Games for All: You May Win a Prize!

3:00: Ride a Go-Kart

4:00: Red, White, and Blue Snow Cone Treats

5:00: Art Projects You Can Do Now

now   may   you   day   see   the   our   ride   boat   blue

Review

WRITE words to finish the sentences.

day	now	you	the	blue

Our car is _____ .

Are _____ ready to go?

I heard _____ dog bark.

Friday is my favorite _____ .

I am ready to go right _____ .

Review

WRITE words to finish the sentences.

| our | boat | ride | see | may |

I can _____ on a skateboard.

Did you _____ that movie?

Ms. Guyer is _____ teacher.

_____ I watch TV now?

We sail on a _____.

now may you day see the our ride boat blue

Review

COLOR the words that are spelled correctly. WRITE letters to complete the words.

o__r   __ou

ma__   d__y

__he   __ee

r__de   b__ue

b__at   no__

Review

WRITE the words in the puzzle.

boat day you ride see blue may now our the

m

y

b   t

r   d

w

mom
was
say
eat
she
look
this
help
girl

but

READ the word. **SAY** it out loud.

I like bananas, but not grapes.

TRACE and **WRITE** the word.

but

FIND the word. Color the spaces with **but**.

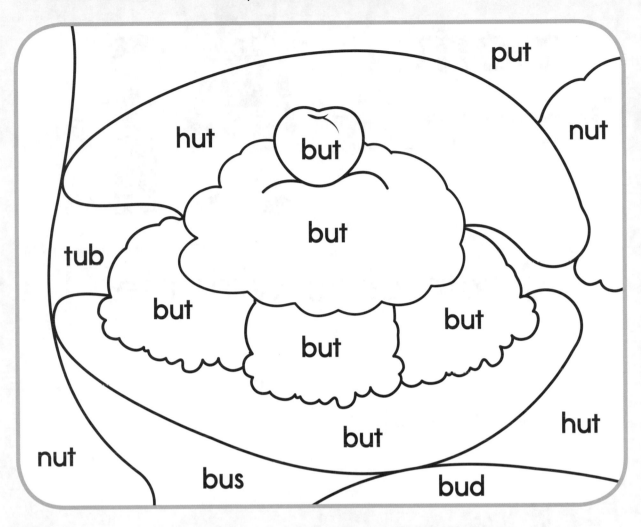

SPELL the word. On each bunch of grapes, circle the letters in **but**.

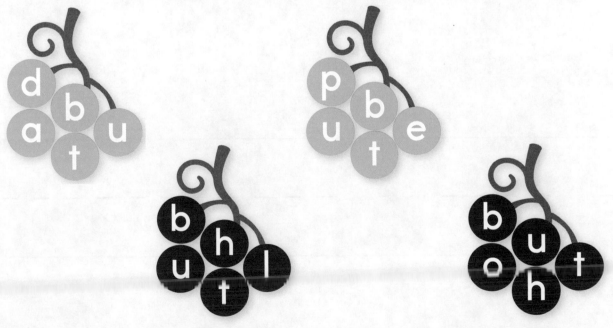

but
mom
was
say
eat
she
look
this
help
girl

READ the word. **SAY** it out loud.

Mom goes with me.

TRACE and **WRITE** the word.

mom

mom

- - - - - - - - - - -

FIND the word. Draw a line through **mom** to see if you won!

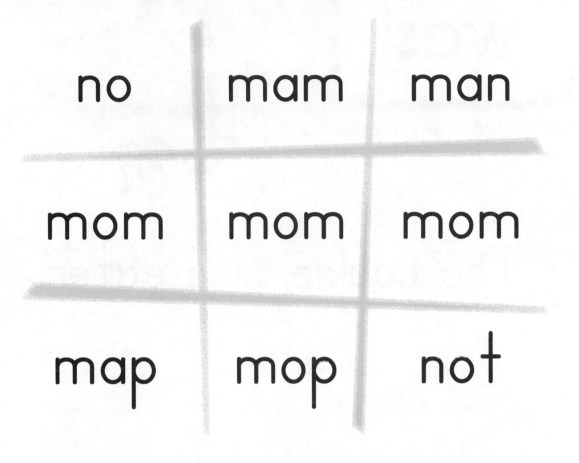

no	mam	man
mom	mom	mom
map	mop	not

FIND the word. Match the shoes with **mom**.

mom

mum

mad

jam

name

mom

but
mom
was
say
eat
she
look
this
help
girl

but

mom

was

say

eat

she

look

this

help

girl

was

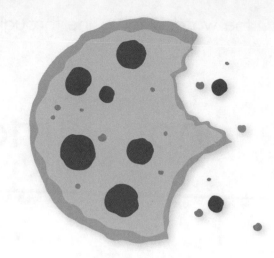

READ the word. SAY it out loud.

The cookie was eaten.

TRACE and WRITE the word.

was

FIND the word in the puzzle. Look ➡ and ⬇.

c	w	a	s	x
e	v	a	w	e
w	a	s	a	w
o	y	m	s	a
k	d	h	y	s

SPELL the word. Write the missing letters.

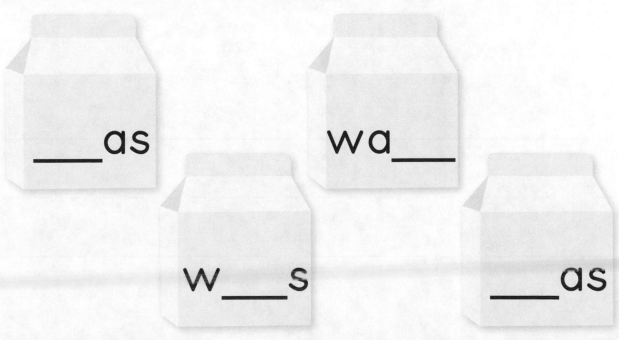

___as

wa___

w___s

___as

but

mom

was

say

eat

she

look

this

help

girl

but
mom
was
say
eat
she
look
this
help
girl

say

Hello!

READ the word. **SAY** it out loud.

What did he say?

TRACE and **WRITE** the word.

say

FIND the word. Color the spaces with **say**.

FIND the word. Color the speech bubbles with **say**.

but

mom

was

say

eat

she

look

this

help

girl

eat

READ the word. SAY it out loud.

The burgers are ready to eat.

TRACE and WRITE the word.

eat

FIND the word. Color the spaces with **eat**.

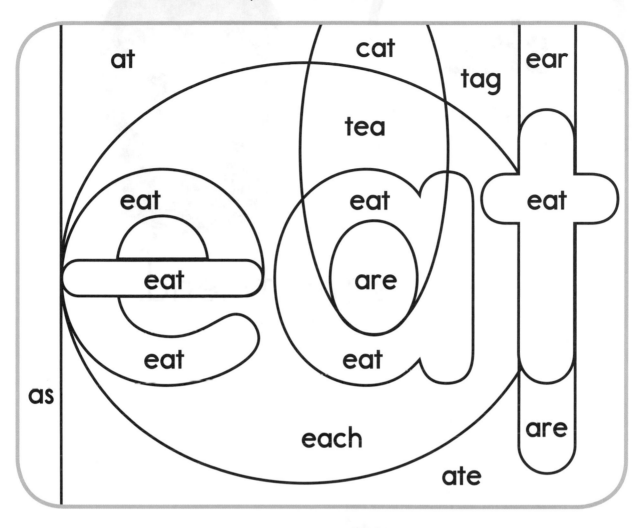

SPELL the word. Unscramble the letters to write **eat**.

but
mom
was
say
eat
she
look
this
help
girl

but
mom
was
say
eat
she
look
this
help
girl

look

READ the word. **SAY** it out loud.

Look at me!

TRACE and **WRITE** the word.

look

look

FIND the word in the puzzle. Look ➡ and ⬇.

d	a	n	o	l
l	r	l	y	o
l	o	o	k	o
n	l	o	o	k
d	s	k	n	l

SPELL the word. Connect the letters in **look**.

but

mom

was

say

eat

she

look

this

help

girl

this

READ the word. SAY it out loud.

What is in this present?

TRACE and WRITE the word.

but
mom
was
say
eat
she
look
this
help
girl

FIND the word. Color the spaces with **this**.

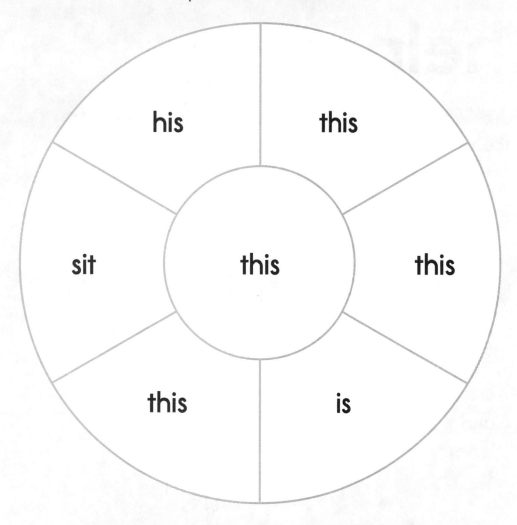

SPELL the word. Complete the word pyramids.

but

mom

was

say

eat

she

look

this

help

girl

but
mom
was
say
eat
she
look
this
help
girl

READ the word. SAY it out loud.

I help wash the dishes.

TRACE and WRITE the word.

help

COLOR each box with **help**. Match each number to a letter to answer the riddle.

	w	e	t	o	l
5	yell	pal	step	hope	help
4	leap	help	well	hen	head
3	help	pale	put	heat	he
2	she	lap	hello	help	plan
1	hat	hear	help	pal	here

What gets wetter as it dries?

A __ __ __ __ __ !
  1   2   3   4   5

but
mom
was
say
eat
she
look
this
help
girl

girl

READ the word. **SAY** it out loud.

There is a new girl in our class.

TRACE and **WRITE** the word.

girl

Sidebar tabs: but · mom · was · say · eat · she · look · this · help · girl

FIND the word. Draw a line through the path with **girl**.

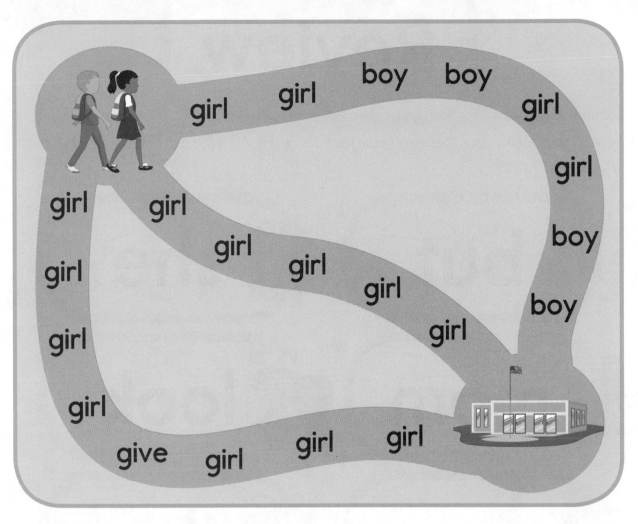

SPELL the word. Match letters in **girl**.

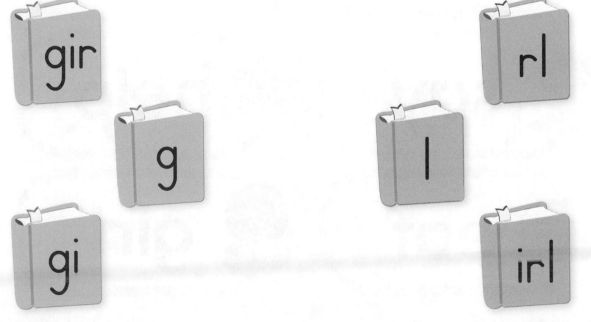

but

mom

was

say

eat

she

look

this

help

girl

Review

READ the story on the next page. FIND the 10 words. Circle each word you find.

 **but**

 she

 **mom**

 **look**

 **was**

 **this**

 **say**

 **help**

 **eat**

 **girl**

Review

What Rose Wants

"Look at this cute goat," Mom said. "The sign says her name is Rose." Mom wanted to pet Rose, but Rose was thinking of something else. Rose pulled on Mom's purse.

"Help!" Mom called. She tried to get the purse back.

I went to see what the zookeeper would say. He told me to give Rose a treat to eat. I talked to Rose softly. "Here, girl," I said. It worked! Rose ate the treat. She dropped Mom's purse.

but
mom
was
say
eat
she
look
this
help
girl

but
mom
was
say
eat
she
look
this
help
girl

Review

WRITE words to finish the sentences.

she   look   was   say   eat

May I _____ this cupcake?

How do these shoes _____?

_____ cheers for her team.

The party _____ last week.

What does a cow _____?

Review

WRITE words to finish the sentences.

| but | mom | this | help | girl |

Put _____ duck in the tub.

My _____ said I can go.

Can I _____ you?

I like blue, _____ not red.

A _____ lives next door.

but

mom

was

say

eat

she

look

this

help

girl

Review

SORT the words. Write each word on a tower.

but mom was say eat she look this help girl

Words with
3 Letters

Words with
4 Letters

_____

_____

_____

_____

_____

_____

_____

_____

_____

_____

_____

_____

Review

FIND the words in the puzzle. Look ➔ and ⬇.

but mom was say eat she look this help girl

s	h	g	e	y	m	i	w	a	s
h	x	a	w	b	e	a	t	h	j
e	c	n	h	w	a	c	d	m	j
s	w	j	e	d	i	p	n	o	x
a	a	q	l	b	u	t	v	m	z
y	v	r	p	f	c	l	k	t	t
d	r	i	y	r	l	t	b	e	h
a	z	l	o	o	k	a	s	v	i
y	u	e	u	j	s	m	g	n	s
w	h	g	i	r	l	c	z	z	j

but
mom
was
say
eat
she
look
this
help
girl

will

READ the word. SAY it out loud.

Will she jump far?

TRACE and WRITE the word.

will will

will
well
four
when
tree
green
that
under
play
like

FIND the word. Color the footprints with **will**.

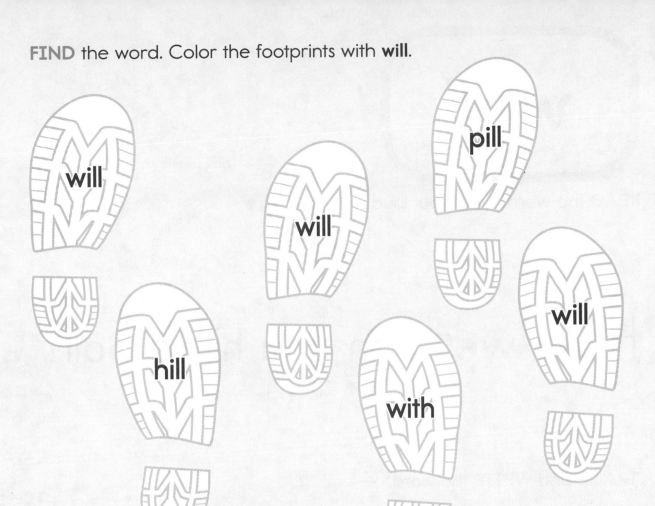

SPELL the word. On each medal, circle the letters in **will**.

will

well

four

when

tree

green

that

under

play

like

will
well
four
when
tree
green
that
under
play
like

well

READ the word. SAY it out loud.

How **well** can you hit a ball?

TRACE and WRITE the word.

well well

FIND the word. Color the spaces with **well**.

were

went

bell

well

we

well

fell

well

will

tell

well

sell

well

well

well

fell

well

yell

wet

will
well
four
when
tree
green
that
under
play
like

four

READ the word. **SAY** it out loud.

I have four quarters.

TRACE and **WRITE** the word.

four four

four

WRITE four under each group of four coins.

_____

- - - - - - - - - - - - - - - - - - - -

_____

_____

- - - - - - - - - - - - - - - - - - - -

_____

_____

- - - - - - - - - - - - - - - - - - - -

_____

will

well

four

when

tree

green

that

under

play

like

will
well
four
when
tree
green
that
under
play
like

when

READ the word. **SAY** it out loud.

When did the rocket blast off?

TRACE and **WRITE** the word.

when

FIND the word. Circle **when**.

when

hen

when

where

when

why

SPELL the word. Write **when** in the puzzle.

h

w

n

will

well

four

when

tree

green

that

under

play

like

will

well

four

when

tree

green

that

under

play

like

tree

READ the word. **SAY** it out loud.

We sat under the tree.

TRACE and **WRITE** the word.

tree tree

FIND the word. Draw a line through the path with **tree**.

SPELL the word. Unscramble the letters to write **tree**.

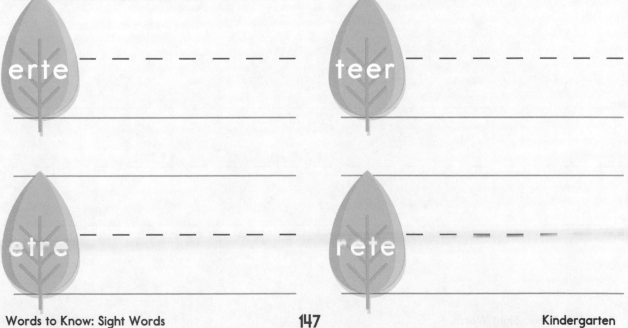

erte

teer

etre

rete

will
well
four
when
tree
green
that
under
play
like

green

READ the word. **SAY** it out loud.

The grasshopper is green.

TRACE and **WRITE** the word.

green

FIND the word. Use a green crayon to color the spaces with **green**.

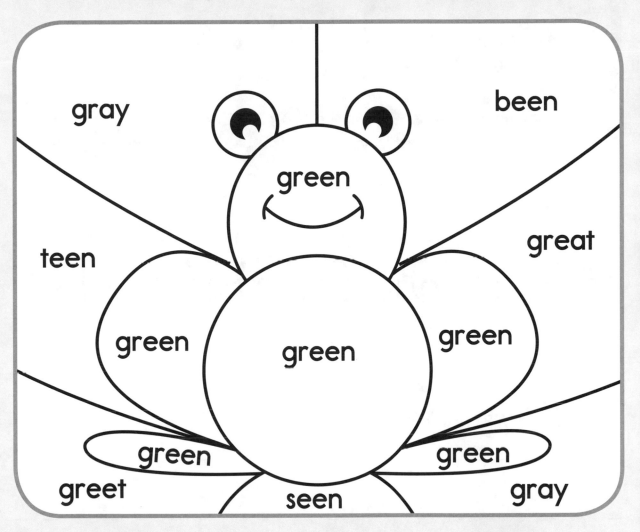

gray

been

green

teen

great

green

green

green

green

green

greet

seen

gray

FIND the word. Match the bugs with **green**.

blue

red

green

green

blue

red

149 Kindergarten

will well four when tree green that under play like

will
well
four
when
tree
green
that
under
play
like

that

READ the word. **SAY** it out loud.

Watch out for that snake!

TRACE and **WRITE** the word.

that that

FIND the word in the puzzle. Look ➡ and ⬇.

c	e	o	k	t
t	h	a	t	h
t	h	a	t	a
t	h	a	t	t
i	h	p	c	n

SPELL the word. Write the missing letters.

th__t

__hat

tha__

t__at

will
well
four
when
tree
green
that
under
play
like

under

READ the word. SAY it out loud.

What is under the table?

TRACE and WRITE the word.

under

SHOW the word. Follow the directions.

Draw rain **under** the cloud.

Draw a cat **under** the chair.

Draw a face **under** the cap.

Draw a string **under** the rug.

like

READ the word. **SAY** it out loud.

I like pizza.

TRACE and **WRITE** the word.

like like

FIND the word in the puzzle. Look ➡ and ⬇.

l	i	k	e	l
m	d	w	q	i
v	a	s	j	k
l	i	k	e	e
l	i	k	e	d

SPELL the word. Unscramble the letters to write **like**.

klie _____

ekil _____

leki _____

ikle _____

157

will well four when tree green that under play like

will
well
four
when
tree
green
that
under
play
like

Review

READ the letter on the next page. FIND the 10 words. Circle each word you find.

 will

green

 well

that

 four

 under

when

 play

 tree

like

Review

Dear Grandma,

   I hope you are well. Now that it is summer, I play outside every day. I found four bugs in the green grass. I learned to swim under the water.

   When will you come for a visit? I would like to see you. We could have a picnic under a tree.

   Love,

   Reggie

will
well
four
when
tree
green
that
under
play
like

Review

WRITE words to finish the sentences.

will well four when tree green that under play like

well	like	that	tree	under

I _____ chocolate ice cream.

This _____ is very tall.

Dena plays the piano _____ .

Where is _____ library book?

Did you look _____ the bed?

Review

WRITE words to finish the sentences.

will	four	when	green	play

Our van is _____.

A car has _____ wheels.

Come to my house to _____.

_____ does school begin?

I _____ see you later.

will

well

four

when

tree

green

that

under

play

like

Review

COLOR the words. Use the code.

Review

WRITE the words in the puzzle.

will   when   play   tree   under
four   green   well   that   like

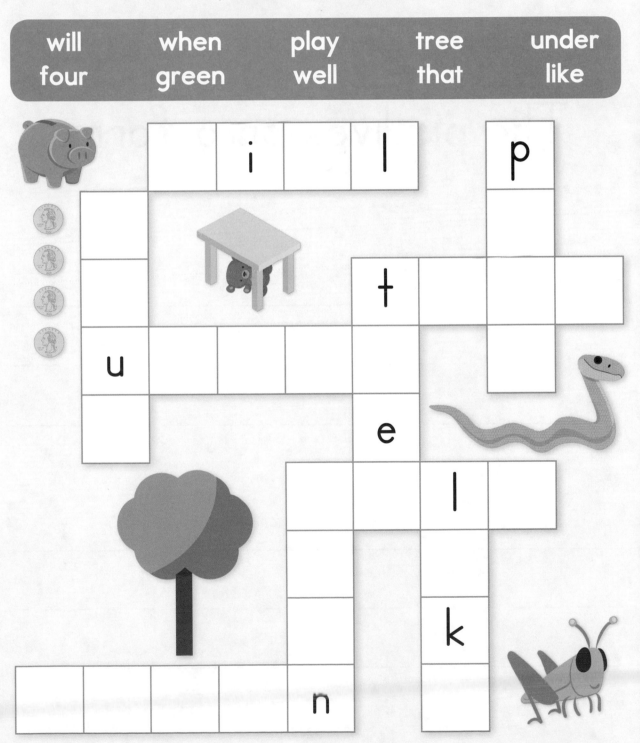

pig
cow
ate
too
farm
want
have
black
brown
apple

pig

READ the word. **SAY** it out loud.

The pig lives on a farm.

TRACE and **WRITE** the word.

COLOR each box with **pig**. Match each number to a letter to answer the riddle.

i   o   k   n

jig	dig	pig	wig
big	fig	rig	pig
pig	pie	pin	pick
pill	pig	pit	hog

4

3

2

1

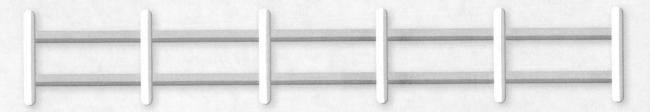

How do pigs write secret messages?

With invisible ___ ___ ___ ___ !
        1   2   3   4

pig

cow

ate

too

farm

want

have

black

brown

apple

COW

READ the word. **SAY** it out loud.

A cow gives milk.

TRACE and **WRITE** the word.

COW COW

166

FIND the word. Color the spaces with **cow**.

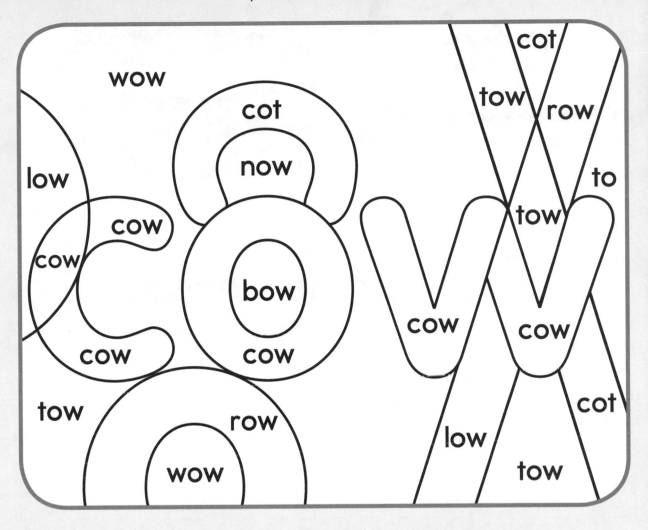

FIND the word. Circle **cow** in each row.

pig
cow
ate
too
farm
want
have
black
brown
apple

pig
cow
ate
too
farm
want
have
black
brown
apple

READ the word. **SAY** it out loud.

I ate some cereal.

TRACE and **WRITE** the word.

ate   ate

FIND the word. Draw a line through **ate** to see if you won!

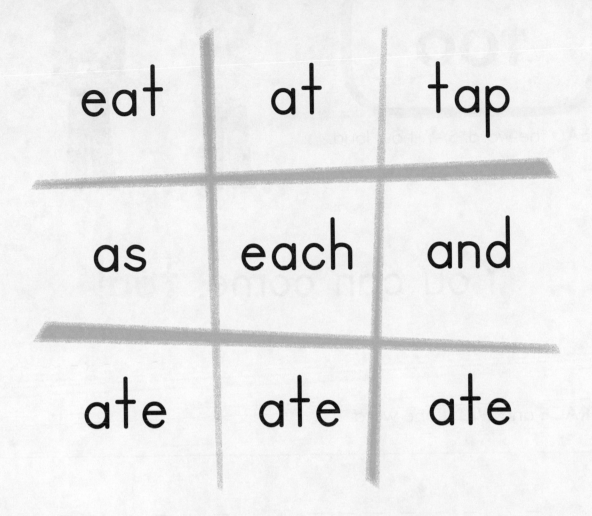

eat	at	tap
as	each	and
ate	ate	ate

SPELL the word. Unscramble the letters to write **ate**.

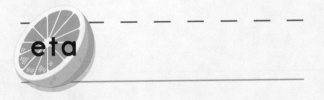
eta

tea

aet

tae

pig | cow | ate | too | farm | want | have | black | brown | apple

pig

cow

ate

too

farm

want

have

black

brown

apple

too

READ the word. **SAY** it out loud.

You can come, too!

TRACE and **WRITE** the word.

too too

FIND the word. Color the spaces with **too**.

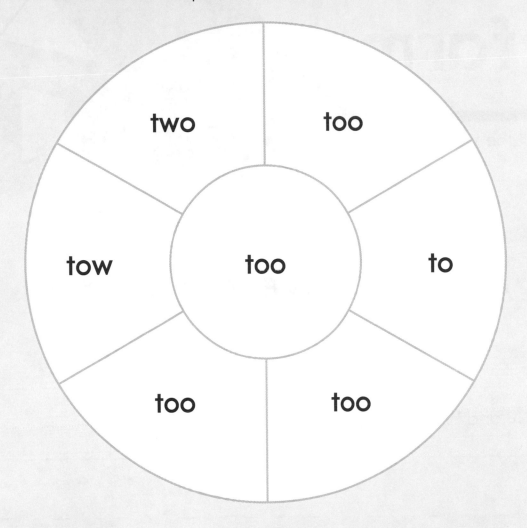

FIND the word. Match the kids with **too**.

pig

cow

ate

too

farm

want

have

black

brown

apple

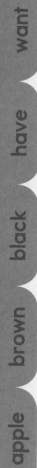

pig
cow
ate
too
farm
want
have
black
brown
apple

farm

Fay's Farm

READ the word. **SAY** it out loud.

Animals live on a farm.

TRACE and **WRITE** the word.

farm farm

FIND the word. Color the spaces with **farm**.

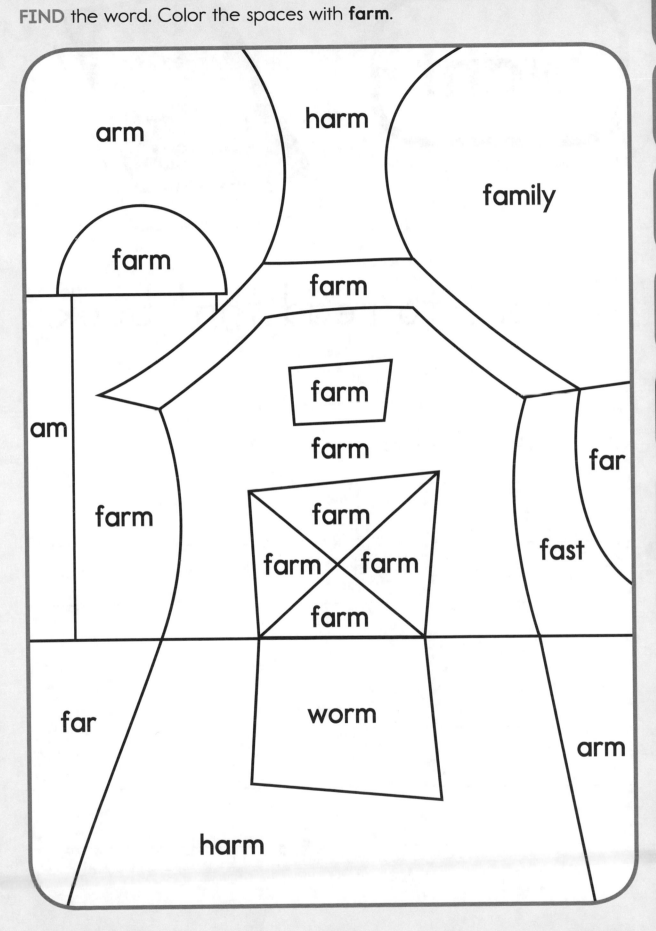

pig
cow
ate
too
farm
want
have
black
brown
apple

pig

cow

ate

too

farm

want

have

black

brown

apple

want

READ the word. **SAY** it out loud.

I want to read that book.

TRACE and **WRITE** the word.

want want

FIND the word in the puzzle. Look → and ↓.

s	r	t	q	h
w	w	a	n	t
a	q	w	s	e
n	w	a	n	t
t	w	a	n	t

SPELL the word. Complete the word pyramids.

pig cow ate too farm want have black brown apple

pig

cow

ate

too

farm

want

have

black

brown

apple

have

READ the word. **SAY** it out loud.

Do I **have** to go to bed?

TRACE and **WRITE** the word.

have have

FIND the word. Circle **have**.

has

have

have

gave

save

have

SPELL the word. Write **have** in the puzzle.

a

h   e

pig
cow
ate
too
farm
want
have
black
brown
apple

black

READ the word. **SAY** it out loud.

Ants are black.

TRACE and **WRITE** the word.

black

Tabs: apig, cow, ate, too, farm, want, have, **black**, brown, apple

FIND the word. Use a black crayon to color the spaces with **black**. Use a red crayon to color the spaces with words that rhyme with **black**.

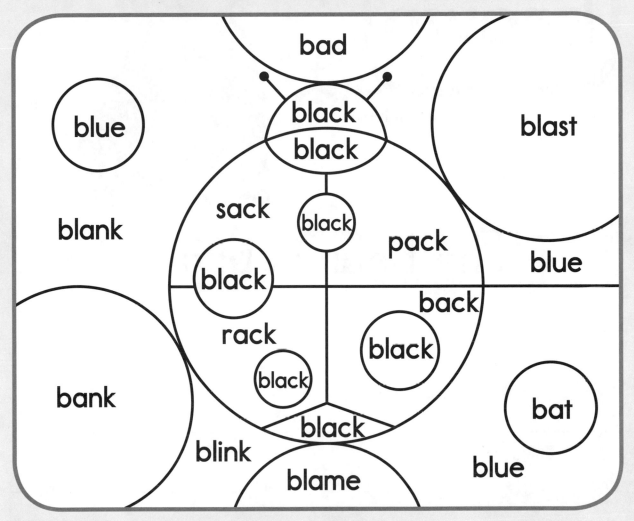

SPELL the word. Write the missing letters.

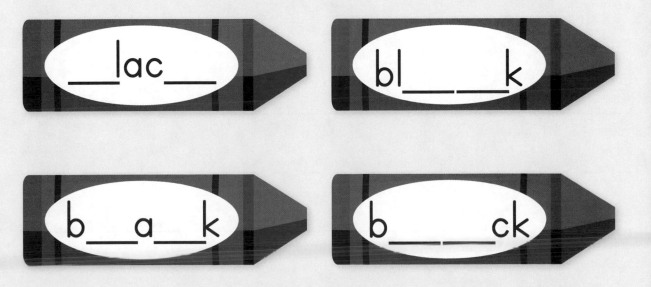

pig   cow   ate   too   farm   want   have   black   brown   apple

apig
cow
ate
too
farm
want
have
black
brown
apple

READ the word. **SAY** it out loud.

The bear is brown.

TRACE and **WRITE** the word.

brown

FIND the word. Use a brown crayon to color the canoes with **brown**.

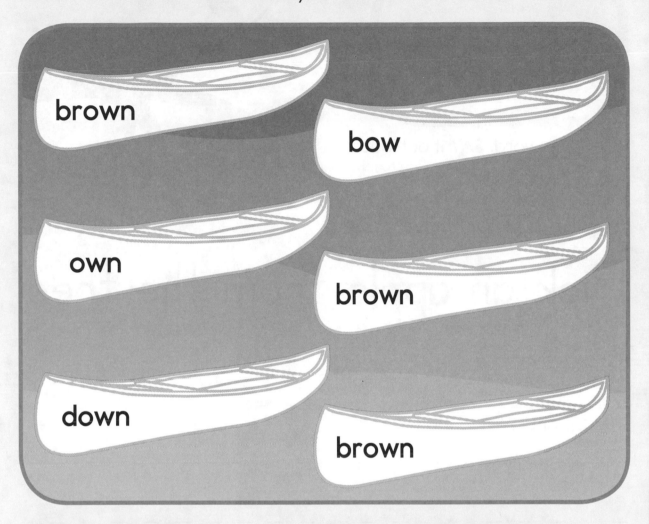

brown

bow

own

brown

down

brown

SPELL the word. Unscramble the letters to write **brown**.

 wobrn

 nobwr

 owrbn

 rownb

pig

cow

ate

too

farm

want

have

black

brown

apple

pig
cow
ate
too
farm
want
have
black
brown
apple

apple

READ the word. SAY it out loud.

Pick an apple from the tree.

TRACE and WRITE the word.

apple

FIND the word. Draw a line through the path with **apple**.

SPELL the word. On each worm, circle the letters in **apple**.

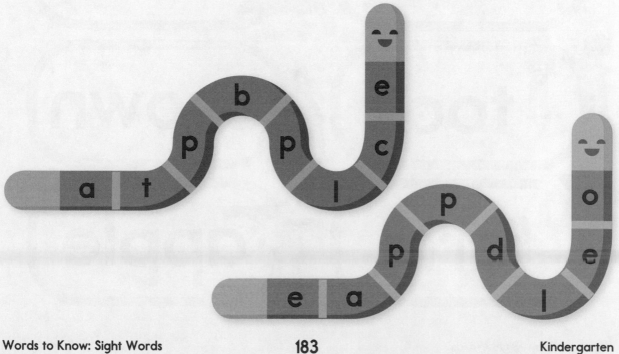

Words to Know: Sight Words

Kindergarten

pig
cow
ate
too
farm
want
have
black
brown
apple

Review

READ the story on the next page. FIND the 10 words. Circle each word you find.

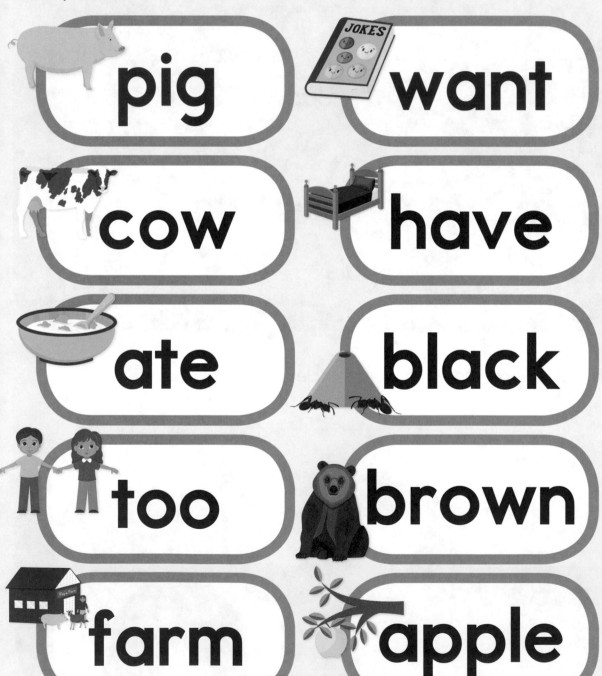

pig

want

cow

have

ate

black

too

brown

farm

apple

Review

Cows Can Hop

"Cows cannot hop, can they?" the pig asked the black cow.

"Cows can hop!" said the cow. He came closer to the pig on the other side of the fence. Then, he hopped.

The pig looked around the farm. He stepped in brown mud to get close to the fence. "That hop was not too high," said the pig.

The cow snorted. He hopped higher. His horn hit an apple on the tree over his head. The apple flew over the fence.

"Now I have just what I want," said the pig as he ate the sweet apple. "Thank you, hopping cow!"

pig cow ate too farm want have black brown apple

Review

CROSS OUT a word for each clue. WRITE the word that is left over.

pig cow ate too farm have apple want black brown

It has double **p.**

It has **i** in the middle.

It rhymes with **how.**

It has **ant** in it.

It is the color of night.

It has double **o.**

It has the same letters as **eat.**

It has **arm** in it.

It rhymes with **clown.**

_____

_ _ _ _ _ _ _ _ _ _

The word that is left is _____.

Review

FIND the words in the puzzle. Look ➜ and ⬇.

apple	pig	want	brown	farm
have	black	too	cow	ate

o	m	h	b	r	o	w	n	o	d
p	j	a	g	n	t	w	a	i	n
i	p	v	b	l	a	c	k	t	p
g	a	e	h	q	l	c	i	t	s
w	a	n	t	t	k	o	c	b	j
a	e	g	x	o	n	w	n	l	r
t	h	h	j	o	a	p	p	l	e
e	v	i	z	w	v	d	u	k	a
s	q	f	a	r	m	g	m	l	x
f	l	p	b	t	a	b	y	j	m

yes

came

stop

then

soon

here

there

where

yellow

school

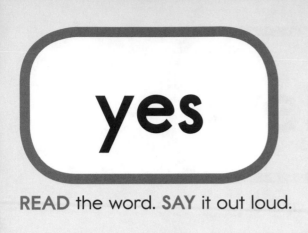

yes

READ the word. **SAY** it out loud.

Yes, I buttoned my coat.

TRACE and **WRITE** the word.

yes   yes

FIND the word. Color the spaces with **yes**.

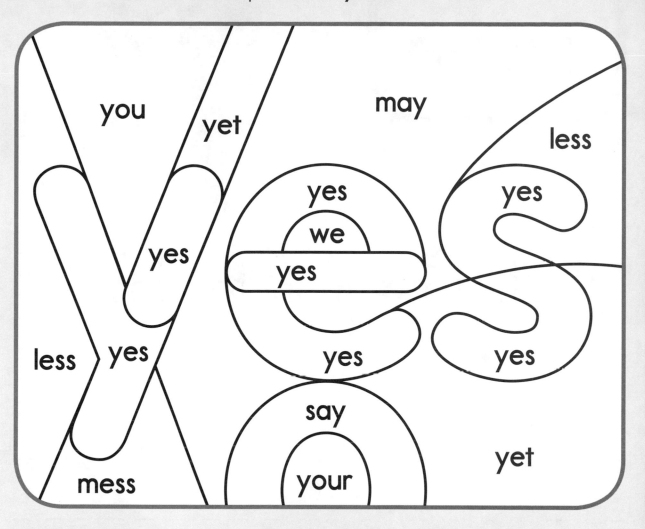

you

yet

may

less

yes

we

yes

yes

yes

less

yes

yes

yes

say

your

mess

yet

SPELL the word. Circle **yes**.

yas

yes

yess

yes

yes

yese

yes
came
stop
then
soon
here
there
where
yellow
school

yes
came
stop
then
soon
here
there
where
yellow
school

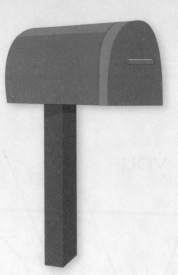

READ the word. **SAY** it out loud.

What came in the mail?

TRACE and **WRITE** the word.

came

FIND the word. Circle **came**.

came

name

came

can

camp

came

SPELL the word. Write **came** in the puzzle.

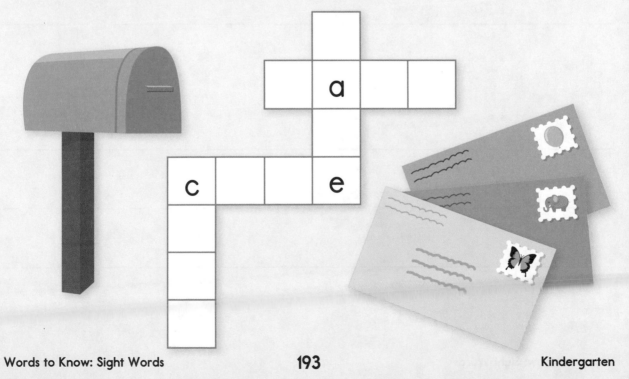

a

c | | | e

yes
came
stop
then
soon
here
there
where
yellow
school

yes
came
stop
then
soon
here
there
where
yellow
school

READ the word. **SAY** it out loud.

Stop at the sign.

TRACE and **WRITE** the word.

stop stop

FIND the word. Circle **stop**.

stop | top
star | stop
strap | stop

SPELL the word. Complete the word pyramids.

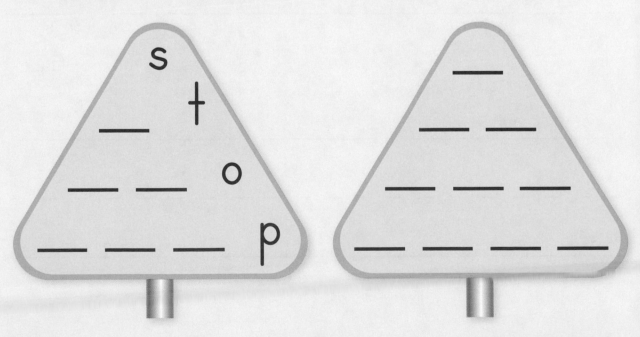

s
_ t
_ _ o
_ _ _ p

—
_ _
_ _ _
_ _ _ _

yes came stop then soon here there where yellow school

then

READ the word. **SAY** it out loud.

If it is windy, then fly a kite!

TRACE and **WRITE** the word.

then then

FIND the word. Draw a line through **then** to see if you won!

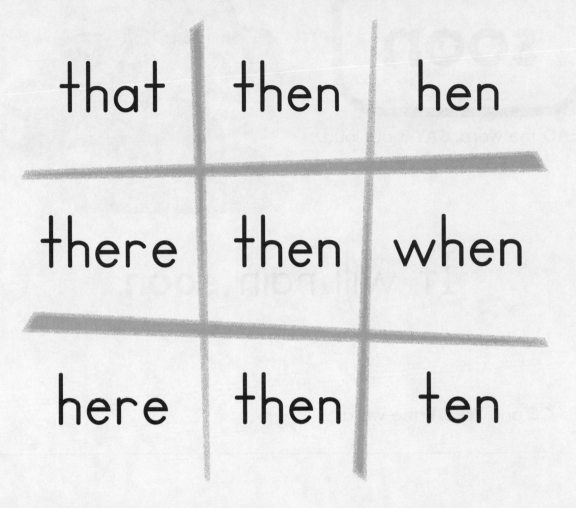

that | then | hen
there | then | when
here | then | ten

SPELL the word. On each kite tail, circle the letters in **then**.

t l h c e n

l t h e n h

yes

came

stop

then

soon

here

there

where

yellow

school

yes | came | stop | then | soon | here | there | where | yellow | school

soon

READ the word. **SAY** it out loud.

It will rain **soon.**

TRACE and **WRITE** the word.

soon soon

198

FIND the word in the puzzle. Look → and ↓.

s	h	r	x	s
o	b	p	q	o
o	g	b	e	o
n	s	o	o	n
r	s	o	o	n

SPELL the word. Write the missing letters.

_oon

__on

s_on

so__

yes   came   stop   then   soon   here   there   where   yellow   school

here

READ the word. **SAY** it out loud.

BUS STOP
CD TRANSIT
Routes: 2B • 4U

The bus stops here.

TRACE and **WRITE** the word.

here here

FIND the word. Color the spaces with **here**.

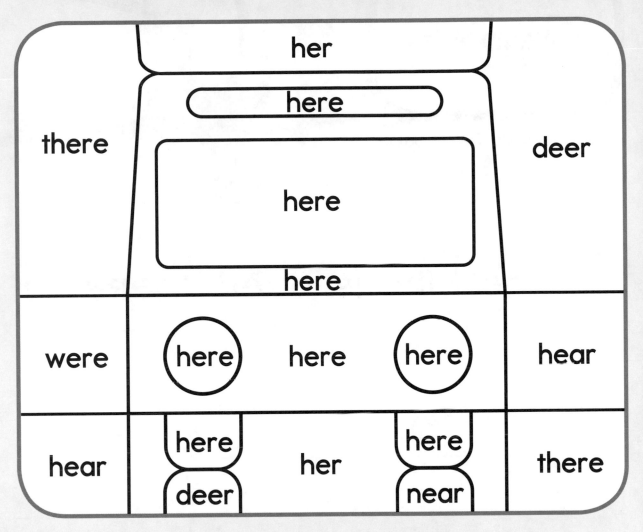

her

here

there · here · deer

here

were · here · here · hear

hear · here/deer · her · here/near · there

SPELL the word. Connect the letters in **here**.

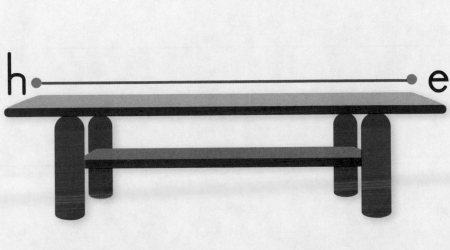

e ·　　　　· r

h ·———————· e

BUS STOP
CD TRANSIT
Routes: 2B · 4U

yes
came
stop
then
soon
here
there
where
yellow
school

there

READ the word. **SAY** it out loud.

The bird is over there.

TRACE and **WRITE** the word.

there

FIND the word. Color the spaces with **there**.

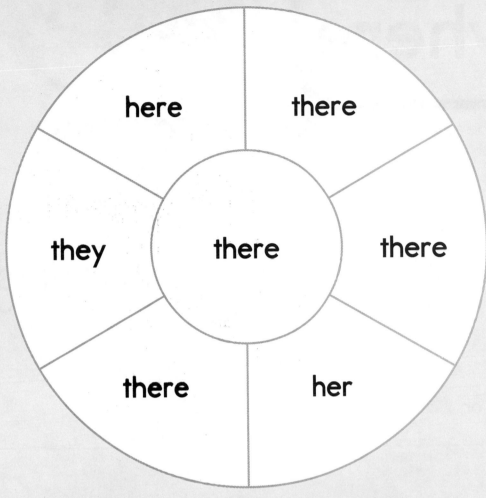

SPELL the word. Unscramble the letters to write **there**.

hrete

rhtee

ehetr

terhe

yes   came   stop   then   soon   here   there   where   yellow   school

yes
came
stop
then
soon
here
there
where
yellow
school

where

READ the word. **SAY** it out loud.

Where is the crab going?

TRACE and **WRITE** the word.

where

COLOR each box with **where**. Match each number to a letter to answer the riddle.

	n	i	t	s	k
5	here	were	there	her	where
4	where	we	when	he	what
3	why	where	hear	wheel	well
2	whale	which	where	while	she
1	help	red	went	where	white

What do you call a smelly fish?

A __ __ __ __ __ ray!
   1 2 3 4 5

yes   came   stop   then   soon   here   there   where   yellow   school

yes
came
stop
then
soon
here
there
where
yellow
school

yellow

READ the word. **SAY** it out loud.

The pencil is yellow.

TRACE and **WRITE** the word.

yellow

FIND the word. Use a yellow crayon to color the ducks with **yellow**.

FIND the word. Match the leaves with **yellow**.

Words to Know: Sight Words

207

Kindergarten

yes came stop then soon here there where yellow school

school

READ the word. **SAY** it out loud.

It is time for school.

TRACE and **WRITE** the word.

school

FIND the word. Draw a line through **school** to see if you won!

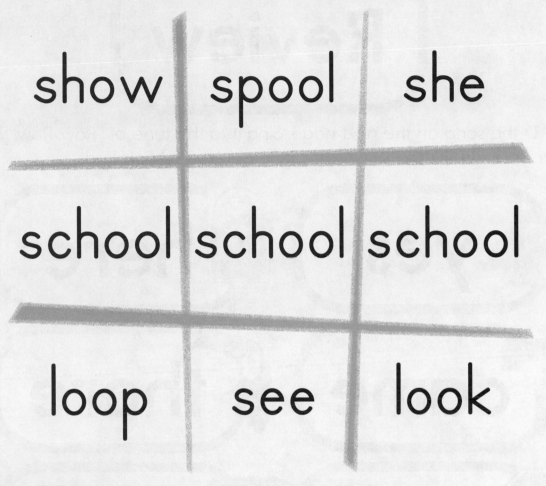

show	spool	she
school	school	school
loop	see	look

SPELL the word. Unscramble the letters to write **school**.

chools _____

- -

_____

slohco _____

- -

_____

Review

READ the song on the next page. Sing it to the tune of "Row, Row, Row Your Boat." **FIND** the 10 words. Circle each word you find.

yes

 here

came

 there

stop

 where

then

yellow

soon

school

Review

The School Bus

This is where the bus will stop.
So soon it will be here!
Then I will ride on the yellow bus
Until my school is near.

There at school I learned and played,
And now the day is done.
The bus came back to take me home.
Yes, riding the bus is fun!

yes came stop then soon here there where yellow school

Review

WRITE words to finish the sentences.

_____ comes the superhero!

Did you say _____ or no?

It will _____ be time to go.

First we eat, _____ we play.

Grandpa _____ on Tuesday.

Words to Know: Sight Words

Kindergarten

Review

WRITE words to finish the sentences.

| stop | school | there | where | yellow |

_____

I want _____ mustard.

She waited at the bus _____.

_____ are 20 crayons.

_____ did you find that?

_____ starts today.

yes   came   stop   then   soon   here   there   where   yellow   school

yes
came
stop
then
soon
here
there
where
yellow
school

Review

COLOR the words that are spelled correctly. WRITE letters to complete the words.

scool
came
thene
there
yes
thair
yellow
soon
here
where
whar
stup
heer
yallow
stop
yas
caeme
then
sohn
school

th__re   ca__e

yello__   s__op

y__s   the__

w__ere   soo__

scho__l   he__e

Review

WRITE the words in the puzzle.

yes   stop   soon   there   yellow
came   then   here   where   school

over

went

with

into

down

good

jump

sheep

white

pretty

over

READ the word. **SAY** it out loud.

The jet flew **over** the clouds.

TRACE and **WRITE** the word.

over over

FIND the word. Color the parachutes with **over**.

FIND the word. Circle **over** in each row.

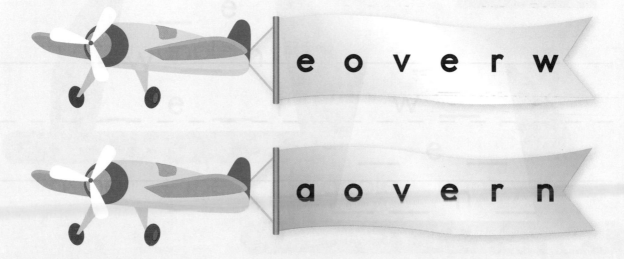

e o v e r w

a o v e r n

over

went

with

into

down

good

jump

sheep

white

pretty

over
went
with
into
down
good
jump
sheep
white
pretty

with

READ the word. **SAY** it out loud.

I like bread with jam.

TRACE and **WRITE** the word.

with with with

FIND the word. Draw a line through **with** to see if you won!

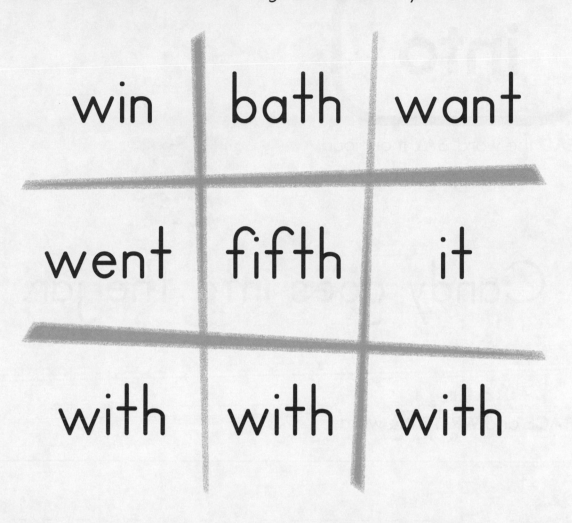

win | bath | want

went | fifth | it

with | with | with

SPELL the word. Unscramble the letters to write **with**.

iwht

_____

thiw

_____

ihwt

_____

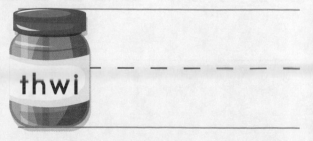

thwi

_____

over
went
with
into
down
good
jump
sheep
white
pretty

into

READ the word. **SAY** it out loud.

Candy goes into the jar.

TRACE and **WRITE** the word.

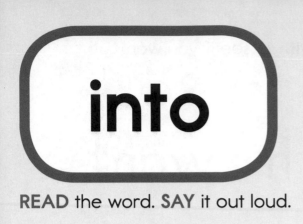

into   into

FIND the word. Circle **into**.

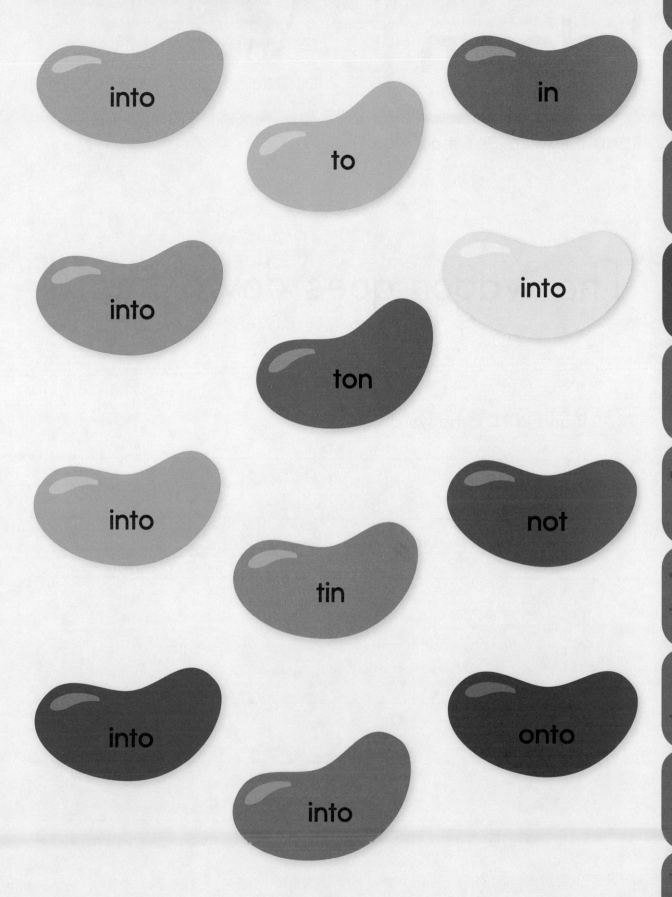

into

in

to

into

into

ton

into

not

tin

into

onto

into

down

READ the word. **SAY** it out loud.

The wagon goes down the hill.

TRACE and **WRITE** the word.

down

FIND the word. Color the spaces with **down**.

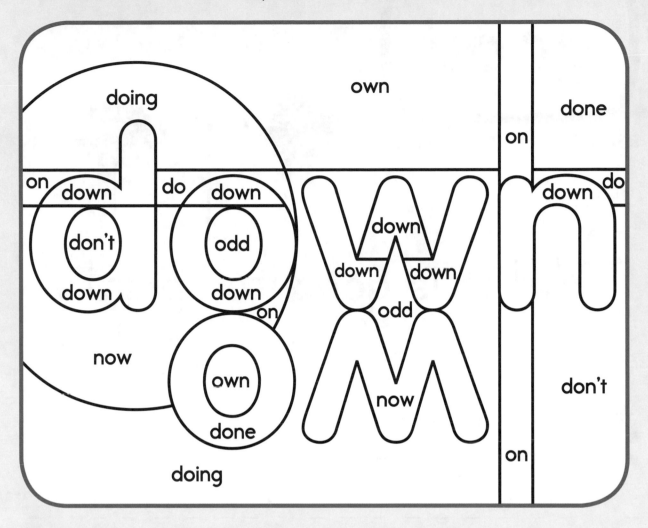

SPELL the word. Match the letters in **down**.

d

dow

do

wn

own

n

over went with into **down** good jump sheep white pretty

good

READ the word. **SAY** it out loud.

Water is **good** for plants.

TRACE and **WRITE** the word.

good good

FIND the word in the puzzle. Look → and ↓.

y	g	j	z	r
g	o	o	d	g
g	o	o	d	o
y	d	t	v	o
k	u	z	b	d

SPELL the word. Connect the letters in **good**.

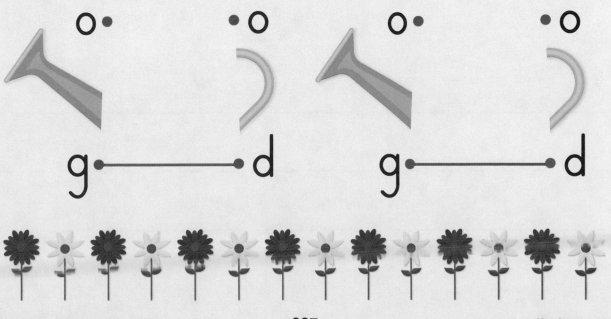

over

went

with

into

down

good

jump

sheep

white

pretty

over
went
with
into
down
good
jump
sheep
white
pretty

jump

READ the word. **SAY** it out loud.

Kangaroos jump high.

TRACE and **WRITE** the word.

jump jump

COLOR each box with **jump**. Match each number to a letter to answer the riddle.

o   c   p   h   u

	o	c	p	h	u
5	pump	up	pup	jump	just
4	junk	jump	jumper	juggle	juice
3	jug	joke	mop	bump	jump
2	jump	bump	jumps	lump	map
1	jam	put	jump	dump	jar

What do you call a lazy baby kangaroo?

A __ __ __ __ __ potato!
   1 2 3 4 5

over | went | with | into | down | good | jump | sheep | white | pretty

sheep

READ the word. **SAY** it out loud.

Sheep give wool.

TRACE and **WRITE** the word.

sheep

FIND the word. Color the spaces with **sheep**.

beep

she

sheep

sheep

sheep

sheep

sheep

peas

sheep

sheep

he

heap

share

sheep

sheep

he

peep

beep

she

white

READ the word. **SAY** it out loud.

An igloo is white.

TRACE and **WRITE** the word.

FIND the word. Draw a line through **white** to see if you won!

what	kite	white
two	white	hit
white	we	with

WRITE white under each white object.

over
went
with
into
down
good
jump
sheep
white
pretty

READ the word. **SAY** it out loud.

What a pretty ring!

TRACE and **WRITE** the word.

pretty

FIND the word. Circle **pretty**.

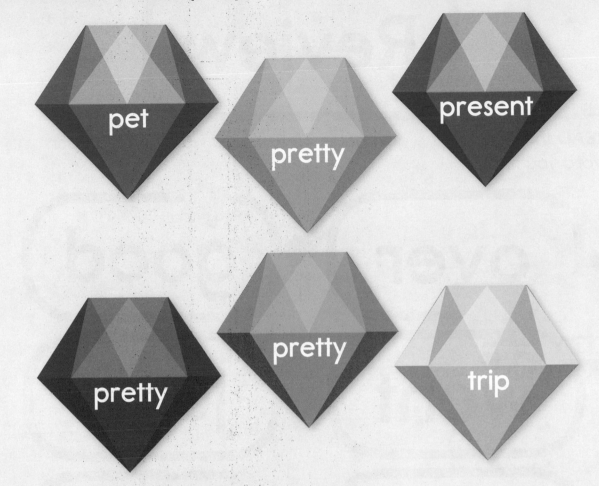

pet

pretty

present

pretty

pretty

trip

SPELL the word. Write **pretty** in the puzzle.

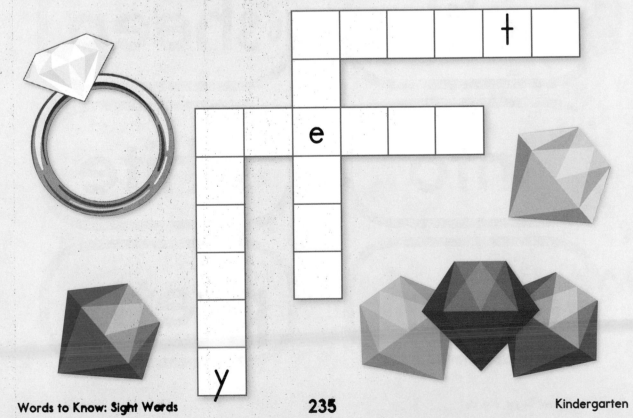

t

e

y

over · went · with · into · down · good · jump · sheep · white · pretty

over
went
with
into
down
good
jump
sheep
white
pretty

Review

READ the story on the next page. **FIND** the 10 words. Circle each word you find.

over

good

went

jump

with

sheep

into

white

down

pretty

Review

The Other Side

Sasha the sheep went down the hill. She saw a stream with water rushing by. On the other side was fresh, green grass. It looked so good to eat! But how could she get it? Sasha was afraid to cross the stream. She might fall into the water.

The white sheep came close to the water. She smelled the pretty grass and clover on the other side. Sasha closed her eyes. She tried to feel brave. Then, with one big jump, she crossed over the water. She did it! Now, it was time to eat.

over | went | with | into | down | good | jump | sheep | white | pretty

Review

WRITE words to finish the sentences.

| with | into | sheep | white | over |

The roll has _____ icing.

The sheepdog herds _____.

Can you come _____ to play?

I will go _____ you.

We jumped _____ the pool.

over | went | with | into | down | good | jump | sheep | white | pretty

Review

WRITE words to finish the sentences.

went	pretty	down	jump	good

It is a _____ butterfly.

I can _____ high!

We went _____ the slide.

I think this book is _____.

We _____ to New York.

over
went
with
into
down
good
jump
sheep
white
pretty

over
went
with
into
down
good
jump
sheep
white
pretty

Review

GRAPH the words. Color one box for each word you count.

over into jump with good

went good good over

with pretty with down

down

sheep over sheep good

white

good sheep with white into

over					
went					
with					
into					
down					
good					
jump					
sheep					
white					
pretty					

Review

FIND the words in the puzzle. Look ➡ and ⬇.

over went with into down good jump sheep white pretty

pretty	down	sheep	over	with
into	white	jump	went	good

z	t	l	g	g	w	f	o	d	m
w	e	n	t	o	h	n	j	o	y
t	a	f	d	o	i	j	a	w	g
y	m	a	l	d	t	u	o	n	p
v	i	e	b	s	e	m	v	a	r
s	h	e	e	p	i	p	e	n	e
b	k	v	i	n	t	o	r	w	t
w	z	u	b	n	w	i	t	h	t
o	h	r	f	c	u	c	i	b	y
p	d	h	z	z	c	q	i	o	j

first

READ the word. **SAY** it out loud.

The **first** rabbit is gray.

TRACE and **WRITE** the word.

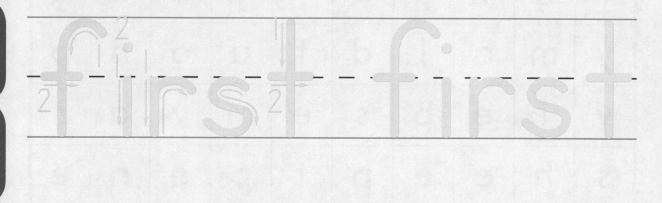

242

they said what away walk little purple orange please

FIND the word. Draw a line through **first** to see if you won!

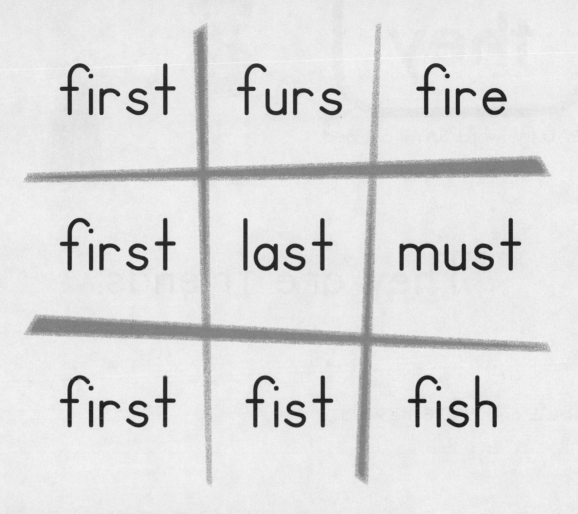

first | furs | fire

first | last | must

first | fist | fish

SPELL the word. Write the missing letters.

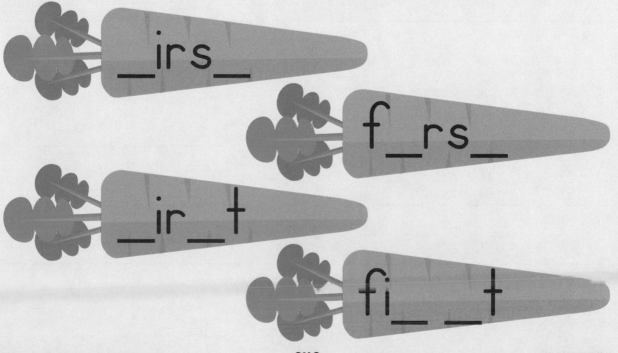

irs

f_rs_

_ir_t

fi__t

first
they
said
what
away
walk
little
purple
orange
please

they
first
said
what
away
walk
little
purple
orange
please

they

READ the word. **SAY** it out loud.

They are friends.

TRACE and **WRITE** the word.

they they

FIND the word. In each pair, circle the mitten with **they**.

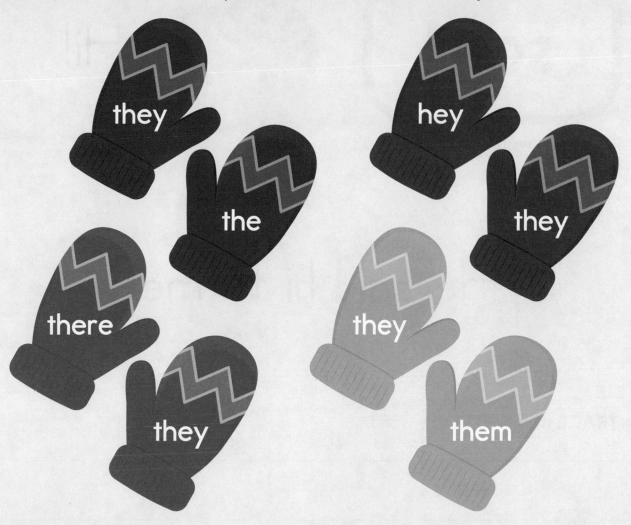

SPELL the word. Write **they** in the puzzle.

said

Hi!

READ the word. **SAY** it out loud.

He **said** hi to me.

TRACE and **WRITE** the word.

said   said

said   what   away   walk   little   purple   orange   please

FIND the word. Color the speech bubbles with **said**.

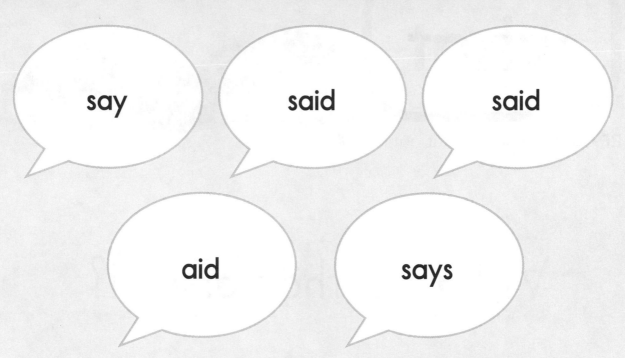

SPELL the word. On each hand, circle the letters in **said**.

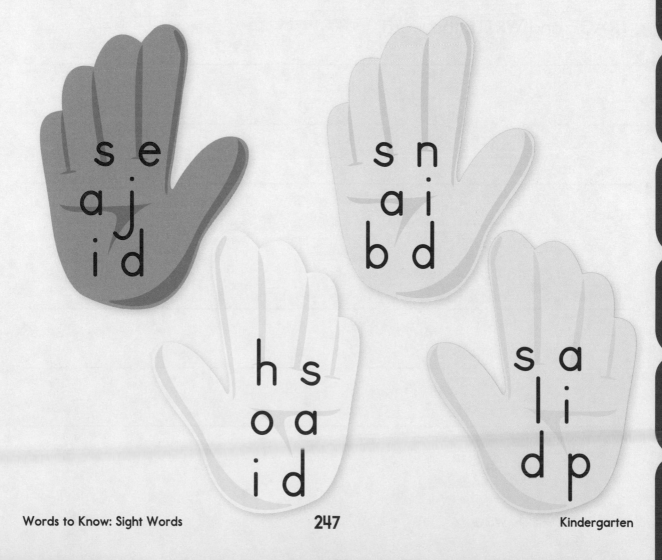

READ the word. **SAY** it out loud.

What is that animal?

TRACE and **WRITE** the word.

what

first
they
said
what
away
walk
little
purple
orange
please

FIND the word. Color the spaces with **what**.

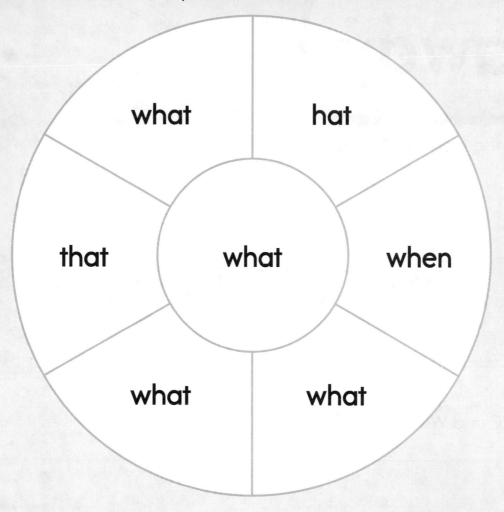

WRITE What to complete each question. Then, circle the answer.

_____

– – – – – – – – – –

_____ are bats?

insects   mammals   reptiles

– – – – – – – – – –

_____ do most bats eat?

meat   plants   insects

first they said what away walk little purple orange please

away

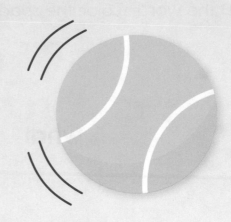

READ the word. **SAY** it out loud.

The ball rolls **away**.

TRACE and **WRITE** the word.

FIND the word in the puzzle. Look → and ↓.

a	t	s	a	f
w	y	j	w	a
a	n	r	a	w
y	y	a	y	a
a	w	a	y	y

SPELL the word. Complete the word pyramids.

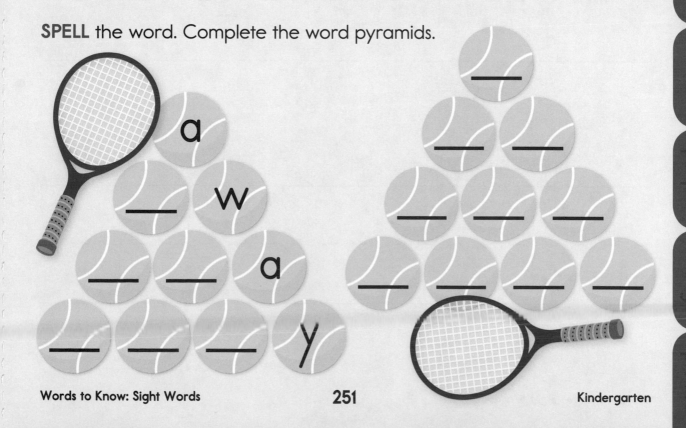

a

__ w

__ __ a

__ __ __ y

__

__ __

__ __ __

__ __ __ __

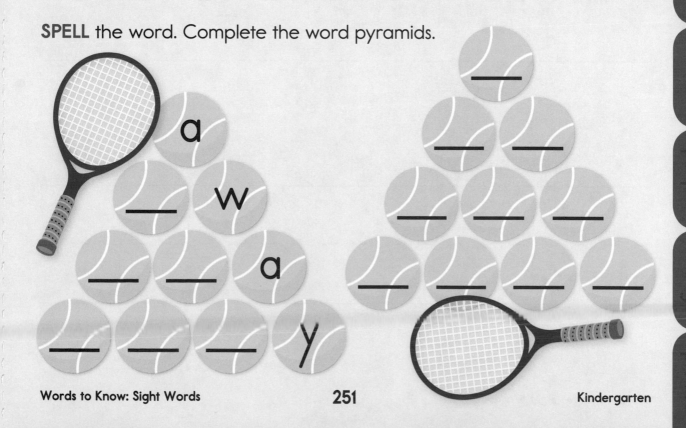

READ the word. **SAY** it out loud.

It is safe to **walk**.

TRACE and **WRITE** the word.

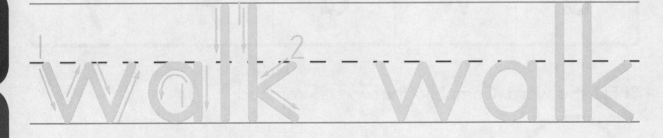

first

they

said

what

away

walk

little

purple

orange

please

Words to Know: Sight Words   **252**   Kindergarten

FIND the word. Draw a line through **walk** to see if you won!

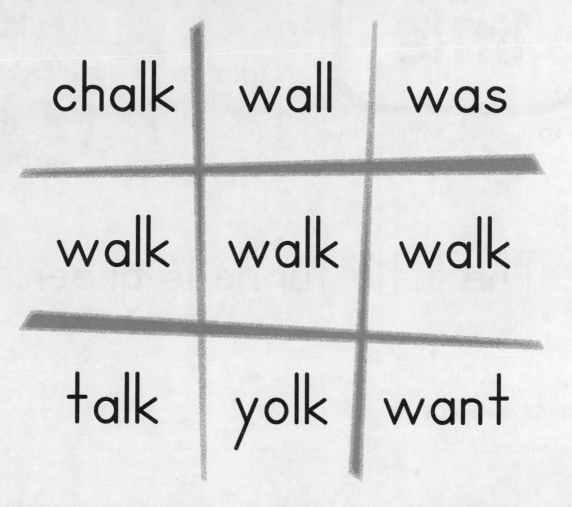

chalk	wall	was
walk	walk	walk
talk	yolk	want

FIND the word. Circle **walk** in each row.

u w a l k f

v w a l k t

w a l k n o

w a l k u f

first
they
said
what
away
walk
little
purple
orange
please

little

READ the word. **SAY** it out loud.

The little turtle is green.

TRACE and **WRITE** the word.

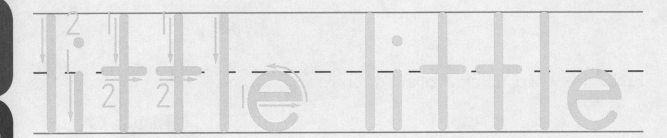

first

they

said

what

away

walk

little

purple

orange

please

FIND the word. Draw a line through **little** to see if you won!

lit	sit	little
tattle	tell	little
let	small	little

SPELL the word. Match the letters in **little**.

READ the word. **SAY** it out loud.

Grape jelly is purple.

TRACE and **WRITE** the word.

purple

FIND the word. Use a purple crayon to color the spaces with **purple**.

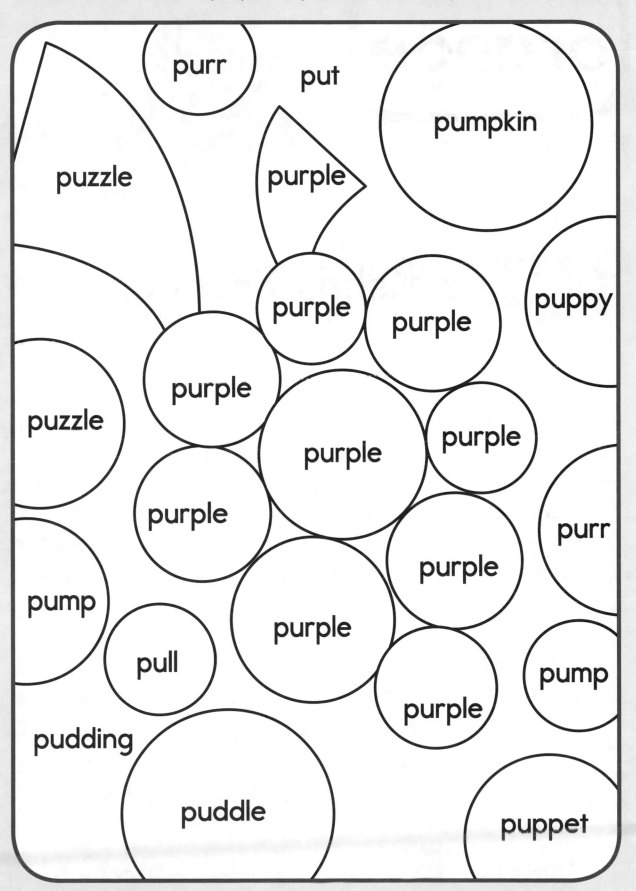

purr

put

pumpkin

puzzle

purple

purple

purple

puppy

purple

puzzle

purple

purple

purple

purple

pump

purple

purr

purple

pull

purple

pump

pudding

purple

puddle

puppet

orange

READ the word. **SAY** it out loud.

The fish is orange.

TRACE and **WRITE** the word.

orange

first
they
said
what
away
walk
little
purple
orange
please

FIND the word. Use an orange crayon to color the crayons with **orange**.

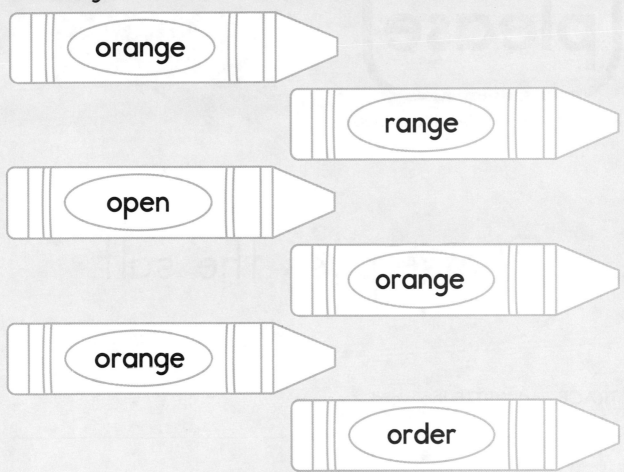

orange

range

open

orange

orange

order

SPELL the word. Connect the letters in **orange**. Color the picture.

r

o

a

n

g

e

first
they
said
what
away
walk
little
purple
orange
please

please

READ the word. **SAY** it out loud.

Please pass the salt.

TRACE and **WRITE** the word.

please

FIND the word. Circle **please**.

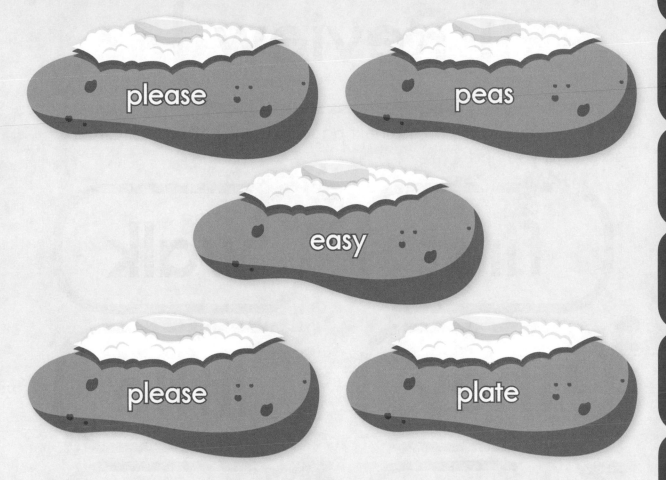

SPELL the word. Unscramble the letters to write **please**.

eplase _____

_ _ _ _ _ _ _ _ _ _ _ _ _ _ _ _ _ _ _ _

salepe _____

_ _ _ _ _ _ _ _ _ _ _ _ _ _ _ _ _ _ _ _

Review

READ the game rules on the next page. FIND the 10 words. Circle each word you find.

first

walk

they

little

said

purple

what

orange

away

please

Sidebar tabs (top to bottom): first · they · said · what · away · walk · little · purple · orange · please

Review

Simon Says

Simon says...

To play Simon Says, please follow these rules. Simon tells players what to do. Players must listen to what Simon said, or they will be out right away.

If Simon says "Simon says" first, do the action. If Simon does not say "Simon says" first, keep still. If you do the action, you are out!

Try it! Read what Simon might say. Cross out sentences that do not have "Simon says."

- Simon says, walk in circles.
- Touch something that is orange.
- Simon says, touch something that is purple.
- Raise your little finger.

first
they
said
what
away
walk
little
purple
orange
please

Review

WRITE words to finish the sentences.

they   little   orange   what   said

I ate a juicy _____.

My _____ brother took a nap.

Ivy and Mo said _____ will visit.

Dad _____ to clean up.

_____ game do you like?

Review

WRITE words to finish the sentences.

first   away   walk   purple   please

My robot has _____ feet.

May I _____ go outside?

The bus drove _____.

We can _____ to the park.

I am _____ in line.

first · they · said · what · away · walk · little · purple · orange · please

Review

COLOR the words. Use the code.

please
little
walk
away
what
orange
said
purple
they
first

little | what
they | purple | away
said | first
walk | please | orange

Review

WRITE the words in the puzzle.

first   said   away   little   orange
they   what   walk   purple   please

Sight Words Review

WRITE the letter on the cherry to complete the words on each ice cream cone.

e

und__r
appl__
ov__r
y__s

t

firs__
s__op
__ree
no__

m

far__
__ust
ca__e
a__

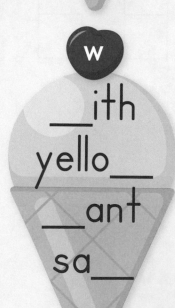

w

__ith
yello__
__ant
sa__

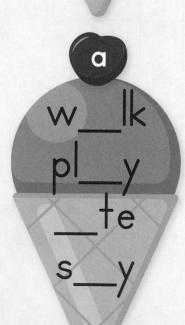

a

w__lk
pl__y
__te
s__y

p

__lease
__retty
jum__
hel__

Sight Words Review

WRITE the letter on the cherry to complete the words on each ice cream cone.

i

g__rl
wh__te
l__ke
b__g

y

da__
awa__
the__
__ou

r

fou__
pu__ple
he__e
a__e

n

i__to
soo__
__ew
ru__

o

t__y
l__k
b__at
d__

d

__a__
goo__
__own
sai__

Sight Words Review

MATCH the words on each garage with a truck.

at be go
he no on
so

was will
went what
who when

sheep school
little all doll
green well

cow
now
brown

cat
dog
pig

out
but
our

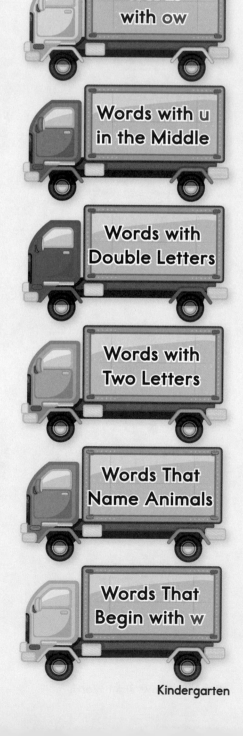

Words
with ow

Words with u
in the Middle

Words with
Double Letters

Words with
Two Letters

Words That
Name Animals

Words That
Begin with w

Sight Words Review

MATCH the words on each garage with a truck.

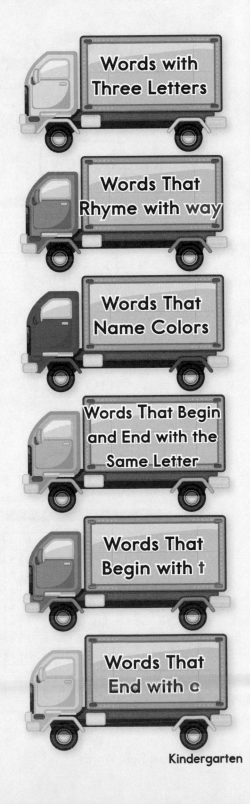

Garages (left):
- did dad mom that
- black orange red blue
- too then this
- may day say play
- ball get eat ran boy she
- ride see there the where have

Trucks (right):
- Words with Three Letters
- Words That Rhyme with way
- Words That Name Colors
- Words That Begin and End with the Same Letter
- Words That Begin with t
- Words That End with e

Words to Know: Sight Words

271

Kindergarten

Review

My Funny Pets

My pets are (so) funny. They (do) love to play. My (cat) will (be) hiding. She waits for my (dog) to (go) by. When my (dog) is (at) the spot, my (cat) jumps out! Then, my (dog) will (run)!

My (cat) has (no) idea what is coming. While she sleeps, my (dog) drops a toy on her paw. She wakes up and they both (run)! It is the funniest thing you ever (saw).

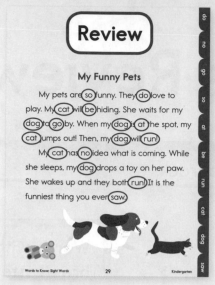

Words to Know: Sight Words   29   Kindergarten

29

Review

WRITE words to finish the sentences.

at   so   run   dog   go

This apple is __so__ good!

The bus is __at__ the corner.

Mom will __run__ in a race.

Can we __go__ to Grandma's?

Why did the __dog__ bark?

Words to Know: Sight Words   30   Kindergarten

30

Review

WRITE words to finish the sentences.

be   do   cat   no   saw

I __saw__ a full moon.

I can __do__ a cartwheel.

This movie can __be__ scary.

Does your __cat__ have stripes?

There is __no__ salad left.

Words to Know: Sight Words   31   Kindergarten

31

Review

COLOR the words. Use the code.

Words to Know: Sight Words   32   Kindergarten

32

Review

FIND the words in the puzzle. Look → and ↓.

cat dog run saw at be do go no so

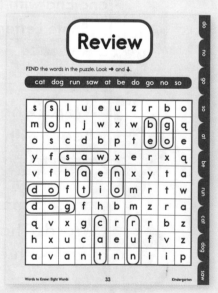

Words to Know: Sight Words   33   Kindergarten

33

Review

(All) My Work

I (did) jobs at home. I took out (all) the trash. I set plates (on) the table. Our dog (must) be fed each day. I (am) the one who feeds him. I got paid for (all) my work.

Now, I can buy a (new) toy. I can get a (doll) or a (red) ball. What do I want most? I cannot decide!

Words to Know: Sight Words   55   Kindergarten

55

Words to Know: Sight Words   272   Kindergarten

Review

WRITE words to finish the sentences.

am	did	ball	new	toy

The keys are the baby's **toy**.

Throw the **ball** to me.

I got a **new** book to read.

Did you eat lunch yet?

I **am** six years old.

Words to Know: Sight Words 56 Kindergarten

56

Review

WRITE words to finish the sentences.

on	all	doll	must	red

The fire truck is **red**.

We ate **all** the popcorn.

Put your coat **on**.

I **must** water the flowers.

The **doll** has a pink dress.

Words to Know: Sight Words 57 Kindergarten

57

Review

CROSS OUT a word for each clue. WRITE the word that is left over.

It begins and ends with the same letter.

It names a color.

It begins with **b**.

It ends with **y**.

It rhymes with **dust**.

It is **no** backward.

It means "every one."

It begins with **do**.

It is **ma** backward.

The word that is left is **new**.

Words to Know: Sight Words 58 Kindergarten

58

Review

WRITE the words in the puzzle.

on	am	did	red	new	all	ball	doll	toy	must

```
a       b a l l
m u s t  o n
      y  d i d
      a  o
      l  l
      l  n
         r e d
         w
```

Words to Know: Sight Words 59 Kindergarten

59

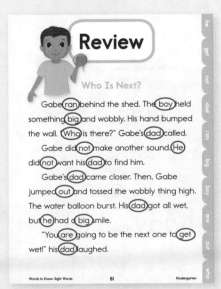

Review

Who Is Next?

Gabe (ran) behind the shed. The (boy) held something (big) and wobbly. His hand bumped the wall. "(Who) is there?" Gabe's (dad) called.

Gabe did (not) make another sound. (He) did (not) want his (dad) to find him.

Gabe's (dad) came closer. Then, Gabe jumped (out) and tossed the wobbly thing high. The water balloon burst. His (dad) got all wet, but (he) had a (big) smile.

"You (are) going to be the next one to (get) wet!" his (dad) laughed.

Words to Know: Sight Words 81 Kindergarten

81

Review

WRITE words to finish the sentences.

get	boy	out	not	ran

Can we **get** pizza for dinner?

It is **not** time to go yet.

We **ran** as fast as we could.

Oliver is a **boy** in my class.

Fluffy got **out** of his cage.

Words to Know: Sight Words 82 Kindergarten

82

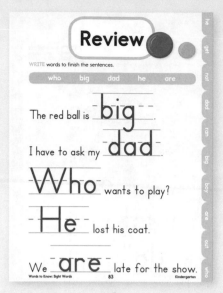

83

84

85

107

108

109

110

111

133

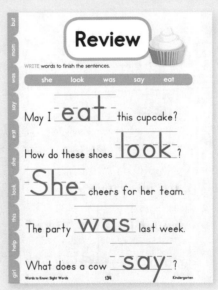

134

135

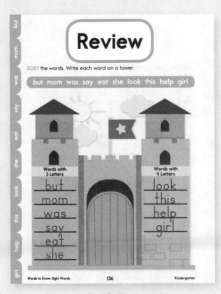

136

137

159

160

161

162

163

Review

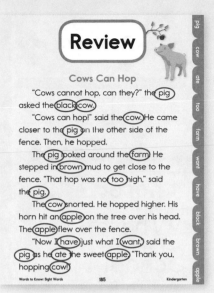

Cows Can Hop

"Cows cannot hop, can they?" the (pig) asked the (black) (cow.)

"Cows can hop!" said the (cow.) He came closer to the (pig) on the other side of the fence. Then, he hopped.

The (pig) looked around the (farm.) He stepped in (brown) mud to get close to the fence. "That hop was not (too) high," said the (pig.)

The (cow) snorted. He hopped higher. His horn hit an (apple) on the tree over his head. The (apple) flew over the fence.

"Now I (have) just what I (want,)" said the (pig) as he (ate) the sweet (apple.) "Thank you, hopping (cow!)"

Words to Know: Sight Words 185 Kindergarten

185

Review

WRITE words to finish the sentences.

| have | cow | ate | farm | brown |

The rabbit has **brown** fur.

A **cow** eats grass.

I **have** three dollars.

Our class visited a **farm**.

We **ate** tacos for dinner.

Words to Know: Sight Words 186 Kindergarten

186

Review

WRITE words to finish the sentences.

| pig | too | want | black | apple |

This **black** hat is magic.

Can I come, **too**?

I **want** to see that movie.

I love **apple** pie!

A baby **pig** is a piglet.

Words to Know: Sight Words 187 Kindergarten

187

Review

CROSS OUT a word for each clue. WRITE the word that is left over.

It has double p.

It has i in the middle.

It rhymes with how.

It has ant in it.

It is the color of night.

It has double o.

It has the same letters as eat.

It has arm in it.

It rhymes with clown.

The word that is left is **have**

Words to Know: Sight Words 188 Kindergarten

188

Review

FIND the words in the puzzle. Look → and ↓.

| apple | pig | want | brown | farm |
| have | black | too | cow | ate |

o	m	h	b	r	o	w	n	o	d
p	j	a	g	n	t	w	a	i	n
i	p	v	b	l	a	c	k	t	p
g	a	e	h	q	l	c	i	t	s
w	a	n	t	t	k	o	c	b	j
a	e	g	x	o	n	w	n	l	r
t	h	h	j	o	a	p	p	l	e
e	v	i	z	w	v	d	u	k	a
s	q	f	a	r	m	g	m	l	x
f	l	p	b	u	b	y	j	m

Words to Know: Sight Words 189 Kindergarten

189

Review

The (School) Bus

This is (where) the bus will (stop.)
So (soon) it will be (here.)
(Then) I will ride on the (yellow) bus
Until my (school) is near.

(There) at (school) I learned and played,
And now the day is done.
The bus (came) back to take me home.
(Yes,) riding the bus is fun!

Words to Know: Sight Words 211 Kindergarten

211

Review

WRITE words to finish the sentences.

| soon | here | yes | came | then |

Here comes the superhero!

Did you say **yes** or no?

It will **soon** be time to go.

First we eat, **then** we play.

Grandpa **came** on Tuesday.

Words to Know: Sight Words 212 Kindergarten

212

Review

WRITE words to finish the sentences.

| stop | school | there | where | yellow |

I want **yellow** mustard.

She waited at the bus **stop**.

There are 20 crayons.

Where did you find that?

School starts today.

Words to Know: Sight Words 213 Kindergarten

213

Review

COLOR the words that are spelled correctly. WRITE letters to complete the words.

scool, came, thene, there, yes, thair, here, yellow, whar, soon, where, stup, heer, yas, yallow, caeme, then, sohn, school

th**e**re — ca**m**e
yello**w** — s**t**op
y**e**s — the**n**
w**h**ere — soo**n**
scho**o**l — he**r**e

Words to Know: Sight Words 214 Kindergarten

214

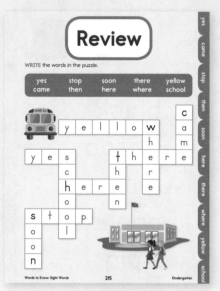

Review

WRITE the words in the puzzle.

| yes | stop | soon | there | yellow |
| came | then | here | where | school |

```
                              c
  y e l l o w                 a
          h                   m
y e s     t h e r e           e
          c       h
          h e r e n
          o
s t o p   o
o         l
o
n
```

Words to Know: Sight Words 215 Kindergarten

215

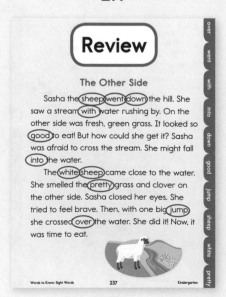

Review

The Other Side

Sasha the (sheep) (went) (down) the hill. She saw a stream (with) water rushing by. On the other side was fresh, green grass. It looked so (good) to eat! But how could she get it? Sasha was afraid to cross the stream. She might fall (into) the water.

The (white) (sheep) came close to the water. She smelled the (pretty) grass and clover on the other side. Sasha closed her eyes. She tried to feel brave. Then, with one big (jump) she crossed (over) the water. She did it! Now, it was time to eat.

Words to Know: Sight Words 237 Kindergarten

237

Review

WRITE words to finish the sentences.

| with | into | sheep | white | over |

The roll has **white** icing.

The sheepdog herds **sheep**.

Can you come **over** to play?

I will go **with** you.

We jumped **into** the pool.

Words to Know: Sight Words 238 Kindergarten

238

Review

WRITE words to finish the sentences.

went pretty down jump good

It is a **pretty** butterfly.

I can **jump** high!

We went **down** the slide.

I think this book is **good**.

We **went** to New York.

Words to Know: Sight Words   239   Kindergarten

239

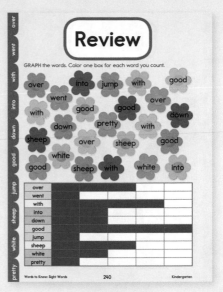

Review

GRAPH the words. Color one box for each word you count.

over	into	jump	with	good
	went		over	
with	good	good		down
	down	pretty	with	
sheep	over	sheep		good
	white			
good	sheep	with	white	into

over	■		
went	■		
with	■	■	
into	■		
down	■	■	
good	■	■	■
jump	■		
sheep	■	■	
white	■		
pretty	■		

Words to Know: Sight Words   240   Kindergarten

240

Review

FIND the words in the puzzle. Look → and ↓.

pretty down sheep over with
into white jump went good

z	t	l	g	g	w	f	o	d	m
w	e	n	t	o	h	n	j	o	y
t	a	f	d	o	i	j	a	w	g
y	m	a	l	d	t	u	o	n	p
v	i	e	b	s	e	m	v	a	r
s	h	e	e	p	i	p	e	n	e
b	k	v	i	n	t	o	r	w	t
w	z	u	b	n	w	i	t	h	y
o	h	r	f	c	u	c	i	b	y
p	d	h	z	z	c	q	i	o	j

Words to Know: Sight Words   241   Kindergarten

241

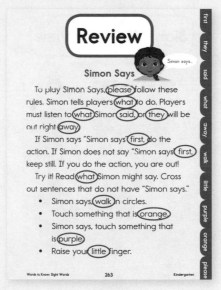

Review

Simon Says

Simon says...

To play Simon Says, (please) follow these rules. Simon tells players (what) to do. Players must listen to (what) Simon (said) or (they) will be out right (away).

If Simon says "Simon says (first) do the action. If Simon does not say "Simon says (first) keep still. If you do the action, you are out!

Try it! Read (what) Simon might say. Cross out sentences that do not have "Simon says."

• Simon says, (walk) in circles.
• Touch something that is (orange)
• Simon says, touch something that is (purple)
• Raise your (little) finger.

Words to Know: Sight Words   263   Kindergarten

263

Review

WRITE words to finish the sentences.

they little orange what said

I ate a juicy **orange**.

My **little** brother took a nap.

Ivy and Mo said **they** will visit.

Dad **said** to clean up.

What game do you like?

Words to Know: Sight Words   264   Kindergarten

264

Review

WRITE words to finish the sentences.

first away walk purple please

My robot has **purple** feet.

May I **please** go outside?

The bus drove **away**.

We can **walk** to the park.

I am **first** in line.

Words to Know: Sight Words   265   Kindergarten

265

Review

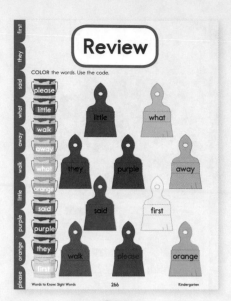

Review

266   267

Sight Words Review

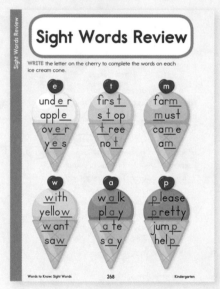

Sight Words Review

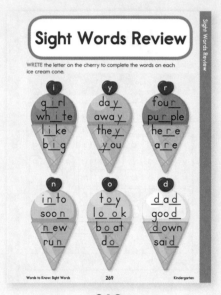

268   269

Sight Words Review

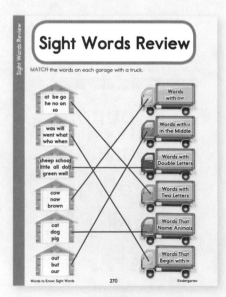

Sight Words Review

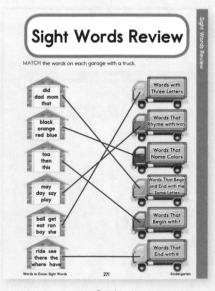

270   271

Sight Words Flash Cards

A flash card is provided for each word taught in this book. Help your child cut apart the flash cards. Store the cards in a zip-top bag. You may wish to laminate the cards or copy them onto card stock.

Use the cards for a variety of fun, hands-on activities. Try these ideas:

Use the color-coded borders to find the 10 word cards that match each section of this book. As your child works through the pages of the section, he or she can match the cards to the activities.

Use the category cards on page 317 to sort all the cards according to how many letters they have.

Put the cards together in different ways to form simple phrases, sentences, and stories.

Find the cards with words that your child can read easily and put them in an envelope. Count those cards and write the number on the envelope. Then, work with the remaining cards each day, moving them into the envelope as your child learns the words. Keep changing the number on the envelope until it says 100!

Spread out 10 to 20 cards face-up. Can your child find pairs of rhyming words? Look at the letters in the rhyming words. Which letters are the same?

Turn any 12 cards facedown and arrange them in a grid. Ask your child to turn over any two cards and read the words. Can he or she find one way that the words are alike? Do they share letters, have the same number of letters, or have similar meanings? If so, your child keeps the cards. If not, turn the cards over. Keep going until your child has all the cards.

Use the cards to play Go Fish. On each turn, ask the other player for a card with a word that has a certain characteristic. For example, say, "Do you have a word with the letter o?", "Do you have a word with four letters?", or "Do you have a word that names a color?" If the answer is no, go fish!

Choose any 10 cards. Then, read a storybook together. Can you find each word in the book?

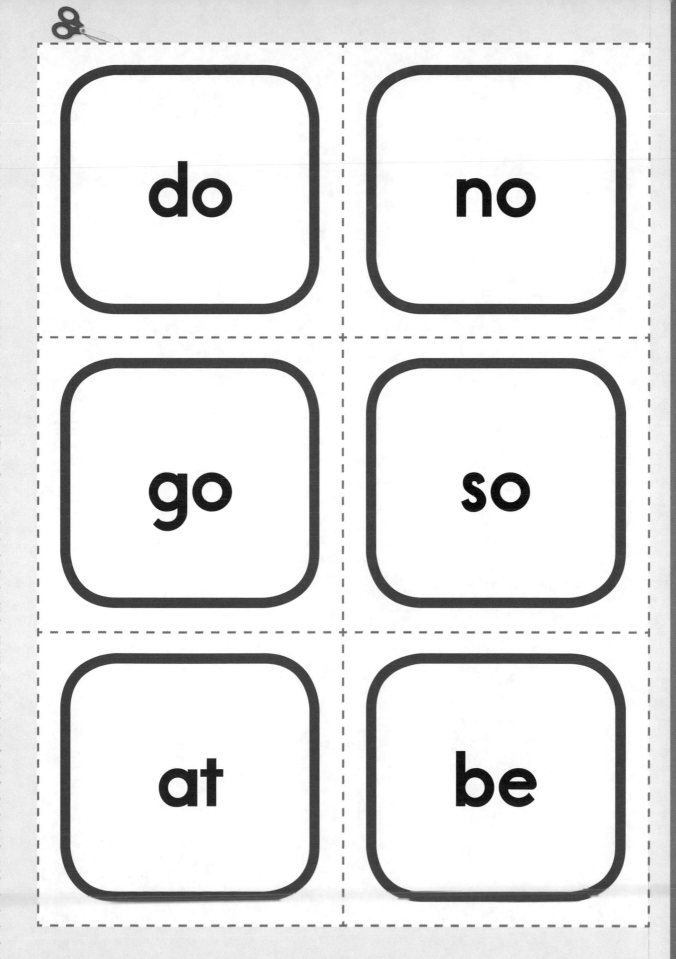

do

no

go

so

at

be

run

cat

dog

saw

on

am

did

red

new

all

ball

doll

toy

must

he

get

not

dad

ran

big

boy

are

out

who

now

may

you

day

see

the

our

ride

boat

blue

but

mom

was

say

eat

she

look

this

help

girl

will

well

four

when

tree

green

that

under

play

like

pig

cow

ate

too

farm

want

have

black

brown

apple

yes

came

stop

then

soon

here

there

where

307

yellow	**school**
over	**went**
with	**into**

down

good

jump

sheep

white

pretty

first

they

said

what

away

walk

little

purple

orange

please

Words with 2 Letters

Words with 3 Letters

Words with 4 Letters

Words with 5 Letters

Words with 6 Letters